OUTDOOR PLAY
in the
EARLY YEARS

OUTDOOR PLAY
in the
EARLY YEARS

Management and Innovation

Second Edition

Helen Bilton

 David Fulton Publishers

David Fulton Publishers Ltd
The Chiswick Centre, 414 Chiswick High Road, London W4 5TF

www.fultonpublishers.co.uk

First edition published in Great Britain by David Fulton Publishers 1998

British Library Cataloguing in Publication Data
A catalogue record for this book is available from the British Library.

ISBN 1–85346–952–1

Typeset by Textype Typesetters, Cambridge
Printed and bound in Great Britain by The Thanet Press, Margate.

Contents

vi   *Contents*

To my husband, Billy, and our three children,
Joshua, Rachel and Esther.

'May you stay forever young.'

Acknowledgements

One of the first lectures I ever had was on the nursery garden and from that moment I was hooked on outdoor play. My interest and love of nursery education stems from my tutor, Jackie Brunner, and so my heartfelt thanks go to her, for opening the garden gate! I was fortunate to work with two exceptional nursery nurses, Deb O'Riordan and Paula Carrott who taught me so much about outdoor play and I thank them.

The photographs in this book were taken at four nursery schools in London (Somerset, Holmewood, Vanessa and North Islington) and The Coombes Nursery and Infant School in Arborfield. I am grateful to Helen Tovey, Senior Lecturer at Roehampton Institute, and Sue Humphries, Head Teacher of The Coombes, for providing the photographs. I am especially grateful for the time Helen Tovey has taken in showing me her collection of photographs and discussing her ideas with me.

Some of these photographs were also included in the British Association for Early Childhood Education exhibition 'Learning for Life'.

I would like to thank the following teachers for sharing their practice with me:

Nikki Everton, Hermitage Primary School, West Berkshire

Teresa Gillen, St Dominic's Savio Primary School, Wokingham

Louise Reffin, Loddon Infant School, Wokingham

Jane Whitehurst, Crabtree Infants School, Hertfordshire.

I would like to thank Professor Philip Gammage, who has always given me support and hope. I am grateful to Helen McAuley and Sue Rogers who have happily let me talk my ideas through. Thank you for listening and not falling asleep! Thanks also to the librarians at Bulmershe Court, Reading University Library for their help, and to David Fulton who has been very patient – I am grateful! And thanks to Sue Coffey (designer, artist and interpreter) for the layout and A-frame design.

Last, but not least, thank you to my family for coping so admirably, and especially to Billy for looking after us all and for reading through my manuscript. Thank you to my friends, Louise Reffin and Malcolm Fleming, and my mother, Joan Straw, for helping out and being there when I needed all of you.

Introduction

A unique characteristic of nursery establishments is their possession of a secure outdoor play area, accessible from the classroom. However, although there is often a will to provide such an area, staff can be unsure as to how to use it and it can often be relegated to little more than primary playtime. This book sets out to take the mystery out of the outdoor play area and outdoor play and to show how to set up and utilise this environment so that it can help in children's learning and understanding. The outdoor play area is a complete learning environment, which can cater for all children's needs – cognitive, emotional, social and physical. It should be available every day alongside the indoor class and throughout the year. Outdoors, children have space, freedom, fresh air and time to work at their current interests. It is an area to which young children are naturally drawn.

Anyone who has spent time observing young children will be aware of, in most cases, their lack of concern for the prevailing weather conditions. Rain or shine, young children want to play outside. Even with a poorly equipped outdoor area, which may have no resources, children will 'champ at the bit' to get outside: they seem naturally drawn to the area. Either young children are perverse, or in fact they instinctively know something which adults seem to have forgotten, namely that the outdoor is a natural learning and teaching environment for young children and is one in which most children feel settled and capable.

There has been an increasing awareness of the importance of the outdoor play area and a desire by schools and classes to develop and improve their outdoor environments (Great Britain: DfEE 1996). This has been so, not only in the nursery sector of education but also in the primary field, for example through the work of Learning through Landscapes, the national school grounds charity (see Appendix for address). The importance of the nursery outdoor area has now been formalised by the Foundation Stage guidance, introduced in September 2000. The Guidance firmly places outdoor provision and outdoor play at the heart of under-fives educational provision. Throughout the document there are references to outdoor play; these include the following:

> outdoor and indoor play should be available, where possible, all the time,
> well planned play should occur both inside and out,
> teaching and learning should occur both inside and out,
> planning should occur for both inside and out,
> inside and out need to be well resourced and well organised,
> sufficient space and time need to be given inside and out,
> regular and frequent physical activity is needed indoors and out.

The Foundation Stage guidance is a good document, which promotes all that is sound in education and highlights play, teaching and learning, independence and no distinction between work and play. In essence this guidance is a description of high quality LEA run nursery education, with early years trained teachers and nursery nurses, providing education and care for under-fives in purpose built establishments. The Foundation Stage therefore, is a welcome document, which can be used by all to really push for quality education. Interestingly enough 11 of the 26 photographs in the guidance, were taken outside.

The success of outdoor play and provision is very much at the mercy of the LEA and the school. Outdoor provision has to be seen as a long-term project, which cannot be rushed, making sure it does become an effective learning environment. Some schools have already created new outdoor areas; some are slowly changing the environment. The challenge now is to make sure that staff observe and teach children outside, and set up activities, which fosters knowledge-seeking behaviour.

So what does and does not constitute quality outdoor play? There seems to be four types of outdoor provision, only one of which constitutes real outdoor play and provision.

1. Primary playtime – this is when children go out into a playground area for a set period of time, either fifteen to twenty minutes or longer after lunch. Children have minimal supervision by unqualified adults, little to occupy them and staff see this as a break time for themselves. This is not a learning or teaching environment nor educational process and although it can be a highly significant time to children, is not given much weight by most staff.
2. The outdoor classroom – this describes an area outside which has been created to house a whole class of children or groups for adult led and controlled activities such as story, singing, or a science lesson. This could be a tree house, a circle of logs, a seating area with pergola and boundary. The area would not be available everyday and used as and when the teacher wanted.
3. Using outdoor features – this describes the process of going out to discover, experiment and discuss the features unique to it, such as the weather, mini-beasts and plant life. The whole class, groups or individuals could use this provision and the session would be adult led and have specific outcomes.
4. Foundation Stage outdoor provision and play – this describes one half of the combined teaching and learning environment of in and out, which involves careful planning and assessment. The outdoor area has grass and tarmac, lots of resources, many activities set up and available everyday for the majority of the session. Children are able to control and modify this environment to help in their learning and interested and well informed adults would work alongside them. There is no division between work and play or a hierarchical division between work inside and play outside. Both the outdoor classroom and using outdoor features will come into the work of this provision, but do not on their own, make the totality of it. Primary playtime has nothing to do with quality Foundation Stage outdoor provision.

Chapter 1 opens the scene with a discussion about the environment in which children learn and are taught. One of the reasons outdoor play does not work is that due attention has not been paid to organisational and managerial issues: how the environment is organised will affect what can be achieved – how we bring children and the curriculum or knowledge together.

One of the crucial organisational issues to address is when the outdoor play area is available. Timetabling outdoor play can have a detrimental effect on the work both indoors and outdoors and so both need to be viewed as a combined space and planned and run as such. Chapter 2 therefore, looks into the combining and managing of these two environments simultaneously. It also looks at the specific needs of the infant outdoor play area and discusses various teachers' approaches to providing outdoor play.

Chapter 3 looks at the roots of nursery education and it can be clearly seen that the outdoor environment is not a primary playtime and was never envisaged as such. Some outdoor areas are more suitable than others, but whatever the space, staff need to exploit the opportunities of the environment and compensate for the constraints.

Chapter 4 looks at features of design and layout which need to be considered to enable outdoor play to work and to make life easier for staff and children. These features include the optimum size, the need for flexible resources and equipment and the limiting effect of fixed equipment.

Chapter 5 looks at how the outdoor area should be set up. The various learning areas or learning bays are discussed as are the resources and equipment that need to be provided.

Chapter 6 focuses on the children using this area and suggests that some children, namely boys, may find this an easier area to work in and therefore easier to access the curriculum here. However, it also looks at how all children should be helped to utilise the area and thus gain from playing in it.

Chapter 7 focuses on the adult's role in planning the area's use and in working and playing alongside children in the outdoor area.

Chapter 8 looks at the ways in which children learn through movement, play and sensory experience. Children at this age want to take on roles and they need to be physically active; outdoors provides the space and freedom to be able to do this.

This book is intended for:

- all those involved with the teaching of three to fives, whether in a nursery, infant or private setting;
- staff in schools, wishing to develop their practice to enable them to use the outdoors to best effect;
- those involved in training or being trained.

It is intended that this book should be a framework within which professionals can analyse their practice and develop their outdoor provision and it draws together much relevant information on the subject. It is also intended to celebrate outdoor play and strengthen the arguments for providing this outdoor learning space.

There is a plethora of terms used to describe the area: 'outdoors', 'the garden', 'outside', 'outdoor class', 'outdoor area', 'the playground', 'the yard'. The pioneers of nursery education referred to it as 'the garden' because it was seen as a child's garden, different from a suburban garden, park, or the playground of the elementary school. Over time this changed to 'playground' as a result of the influence of elementary and primary education. I will mostly use the terms 'outdoor play area', 'outdoor space', 'outdoor area', 'outdoor environment' and sometimes 'garden'.

The Foundation Stage is simply a term used to describe the period from age three to when a child becomes five. The Foundation Stage guidance offers principles for early years education, what might be expected of children at different stages from three to five, and what staff could do to put the principles into action. Throughout this book therefore, I will use the term 'Foundation Stage' to describe this period of time in a child's educational life. I will also use the term 'nursery' which does have two definitions, but I will be referring to the former definition only. One describes the education and care of children in establishments run by the LEA, in mostly purpose built buildings, employing nursery teachers and nursery nurses and prior to 1997 was the only meaning for nursery. However, in 1997 with the introduction of the voucher system and the desirable learning outcomes 'nursery' became a blanket term to describe any establishment catering for children under five, whether it be privately run, LEA run or of charitable status (for example a playgroup). I consider the Foundation Stage guidance is actually describing good quality nursery education as seen in the first definition. The Foundation Stage has now become the blanket term for the care and education of under-fives, and is pertinent to any child in an establishment until their fifth birthday. This will include a nursery class attached to a primary school, a separate nursery school, a reception class, a rising fives class, a combination of reception, year 1 and 2 children, a privately run institution, a playgroup. So the significant change with the introduction of this guidance is the inclusion of reception children in the Foundation Stage and not the National Curriculum.

For outdoor play to be effective and instrumental in children's learning it has to be organised in a particular way, and there are a number of guiding principles which need to be adhered to. The driving force has to be the will to want it to work, a belief in its value and an enjoyment of working outside. Without this the principles cannot work. The principles are:

- indoors and outdoors need to be viewed as one combined and integrated environment;
- indoors and outdoors need to be available to the children simultaneously;
- outdoors is an equal player to indoors and should receive planning, management, evaluation, resourcing, staffing and adult interaction on a par with indoors;
- outdoors is both a teaching and learning environment;
- outdoor design and layout needs careful consideration;
- outdoor play is central to young children's learning, possibly more to some children than others;
- the outdoor classroom offers children the opportunity to utilise effective modes of learning – play, movement and sensory experience;
- children need versatile equipment and environments;
- children need to be able to control, change and modify their environment;
- staff have to be supportive toward outdoor play.

It is to these principles I now turn, to explore in depth how to make the outdoor environment a successful learning and teaching area.

1: An environment for teaching and learning

Blenkin and Whitehead argue that 'the most neglected and misunderstood dimension of the planned curriculum is the creation of an environment or setting in which education is to take place' (1988, p. 35). The outdoor play area of the nursery seems to be one of those areas which has suffered from this neglect. Sometimes it is an area which is not part of the overall planning, is not resourced or managed well, is not evaluated and is an area in which staff do not work with children. Outdoors is seen, purely and simply, as a space, similar to the infant playground. The effect of this neglect is that, not surprisingly, outdoor play is unsuccessful, learning occurs by chance, and what is learned can be very limited and limiting. In this chapter therefore, I will place the creation of an environment, which includes management and organisation, teaching and learning at the heart of successful, quality outdoor play.

McAuley and Jackson (1992) discuss the environment in terms of space, time and task, and argue that all have to be structured and 'reflection on structures is crucial to quality education' (p. 121). Moreover, they argue that 'space planning is a key factor in the structuring of learning contexts' and 'should be compatible in aims and values with other classroom policies and with the philosophy of the whole institution' (pp. 64–5). McLean (1991) talks about the physical environment 'challenging, engaging and supporting children' (p. 218). She argues that the physical environment can have an acute impact on the way children interact. In her study of four teachers, she found the most successful in terms of enabling children to learn, was the one who paid greatest attention to the issue of the environment in planning and provision, and also throughout the session while children were playing. Bruce (1987) argues that 'the environment is the mechanism by which the teacher brings the child and different areas of knowledge together' (p. 54). The environment is, therefore, the means by which knowledge and the child are linked; it forms part of the education equation and as such has to be planned carefully. In other words, attention has to be paid to this part of our work: environment can affect how, and what, children learn. As The Fun Boy Three/Bananarama song goes 'T'ain't what you do, it's the way that you do it, that's what gets results'!

Teaching and learning

A school is about both teaching and learning. Education is about providing both a teaching and learning environment, a sentiment echoed in the Foundation Stage guidance (QCA 2000, pp. 20–24). This means that not only will children be explicitly taught by an adult, but they will also be able to get on and learn by themselves and with other children. For children to learn independently means that teaching and learning have to have equal status, and the environment has to be well resourced and carefully planned. Learning cannot be seen as secondary to teaching and it is not sufficient to hope that children will learn by chance.

Unfortunately, outdoor play has sometimes been viewed as something children do on their own and is secondary to what goes on in the classroom. 'Frequent lack of attention to the external environment must come from some bizarre assumption that knowledge acquired indoors is superior to that gained outside' (Bruce 1987, p. 55). Therefore the very essence of a learning environment has been misunderstood and its effectiveness extremely limited.

For outdoor play to be successful it is crucial that the outdoor environment is considered in as much depth as any other educational setting. It will not be as effective if it is seen as secondary to the indoor classroom. Returning to the principles in the Introduction, the outdoor environment has to accommodate both teaching and learning and has to facilitate both.

It is, of course, very difficult to divide the two terms: teaching and learning. By teaching is meant those times when the adult is giving specific input to a group of children or to an individual, when an adult is teaching a specific concept which by its nature needs an adult to be involved. Children need clear adult input to reach their potential, for example, in movement skills (Gallahue 1989) and this is so in other areas. Moyles (1992) argues that teachers have to decide what to actually teach and what to allow children to find out for themselves alone. Some things are better taught, such as art techniques (p. 123), and some are better discovered independently. She argues further that children can be given more independence if they are taught certain techniques, as they can then choose from a greater range of options or methods as to how to tackle a task. The Foundation Stage guidance talks in terms of teaching helping children 'to make connections in their learning' and to think forward and to reflect (QCA 2000, p. 22).

Setting up an environment for learning means that children can work together or alone and can find out for themselves; it is about implicitly learning and not being explicitly taught. So, for example, learning to care for others starts with adults caring for children, learning to be independent starts with children being given responsibility. It means that the nature of the activity does not need constant adult input, but does *not* mean that adults should not be involved at all. Adults need to accept that children are capable of finding out for themselves and are able to manipulate the environment to make discoveries. The way to encourage learning such as investigation, creativity and consolidation are through play and talk. (QCA 2000, p. 20). The environment therefore, has to be exciting and stimulating so that children are motivated to utilise the resources and learn. This in turn means that resources and activities need to be carefully chosen. It ultimately means that adults must use their skills of observation to know when to get involved in play, to decide what needs to be done in any situation and to note down difficulties and achievements.

Organisation and management

It can be hard to see the outside as an environment for learning because it does not look like a 'normal' setting for learning. It does not have a floor, walls, ceiling, or windows. Probably the easiest way to approach the planning of outdoors is to temporarily view outdoors in the same way as indoors. Pretend the outdoor area has walls and a ceiling, what would you have in it? You would have furniture and resources, either around the room or on the walls, children utilising those resources and the furniture, children and staff working together. Having accepted this, it then follows that the outdoors has to be part of the planning, it has to be on the long-term, medium-term and day-to-day planning grids. It has to be evaluated and children working in that environment have to be assessed. It has to be discussed at staff

Figure 1.1 Milkmen – collaboration and negotiation. (See Chapter 8 for further discussion.)

meetings. So, when working outside, all the management and organisational issues which we would address in the indoor class have to be considered.

Organisation is 'the way in which the class and classroom is structured to facilitate teaching and learning' (Pollard and Tann 1987, p. 102) and includes:

- the way children and adults are organised,
- the use of time, display, space, resources and
- the use of records for monitoring organisation.

Moyles (1992) describes organisation in terms of 'the context and contents of the classroom setting, including the plans made for teaching and learning' (p. 5). Management is the 'action part of the reflective teaching style' and this includes the day-to-day running of the class and the managing of every learning situation. It is about managing time, people and resources and is crucial in ensuring the success or otherwise in teaching and learning (Pollard and Tann 1987, p. 120). Moyles (1992) argues that management is about what teachers do in response to their organisation 'to ensure both the smooth running of the learning environment and fulfilment of intentions' (p. 5). Management and organisation are therefore closely linked and have to be considered daily. The National Foundation for Educational Research (NFER) project which looked at four-year-olds in schools highlights particular issues to do with organisation and management, namely, time, space, resources, the teaching approach, activities, staffing and monitoring (Cleave and Brown 1989). Figure 1.2 lists the factors which need to be considered when thinking about organisation and management of either an indoor or outdoor learning environment.

Teachers:
philosophy
view of the child
ethos and expectations
planning, observation and evaluation
teaching and learning styles
relationships – trust and respect
behaviour management
management of other people
approach and interaction – playing and working with children
expectations of children's behaviour – independence, trust, autonomy, social
understanding
praising
groupings
fine-tuning
parents

Children:
modes of learning
individuals
understanding of and involvement in formulation of values and expectations
procedures for using and moving resources
procedures for getting help
children's self-image
behaviour expectations
movement of children – from indoors to outdoors and between bays
groupings

Time:
beginnings and starting points
transitions and endings
setting up and clearing away
use of children's time
use of adults' time
when activities available, continuity of activities

Physical setting:
use of space
furniture
equipment – static and movable
layout and positioning
resources – plentiful and varied, clearly labelled, accessible
learning bays – positioning, arrangement
boundaries
walkways
surfaces
weather – impact on children and staff and environment
storage
safety
presentation/pleasing/comfortable

Figure 1.2 The environment – Issues to consider

Time

Under-fives need a flexible approach to the day and particularly time to play with few interruptions. If children are part of a class where interruptions are frequent they are less likely to settle to tasks. If they know that they have time to pursue activities they will be more motivated to concentrate, persevere and be successful. McAuley and Jackson (1992) argue that interrupting 'children's absorbed activity' can 'contribute to a culture which is almost as subversive of learning as allowing disruptive behaviour to become a tolerated norm' (pp. 46–7). As well as not interrupting children, it is important that children spend time on worthwhile activities and not on time-wasting tasks. The guidance argues that children need time to play and work, that practitioners need to be flexible in their planning, so children can follow an interest and if necessary enable children to return to an activity at a later time (QCA 2000).

Hilsum and Cane (1971) found that in their study of children in school, a quarter of the time was taken up by non-educational household matters and half in organisa-tional matters, such as planning and marking. The ORACLE project came to similar conclusions (Galton *et al.* 1980). In terms of outdoor play, then, this means children do not need to waste time lining up to go outside, but need to be able to use both areas freely, thereby making sure they make optimum use of both spaces and have uninterrupted time to pursue interests. Staff need to plan it so children can access the outside area as soon as possible after they have come into the class. Staff need to organise their time so that they are free to work with those children they want to, and not spend time responding to problems which have resulted from poor organisation.

Space

Young children also need space, as movement is central to their development and learning. They are not yet at the stage of sitting quietly and learning, but at the moving-about and finding-out stage. Four-years-olds need space as they are very active, both physically and mentally, and also because their motor development is at a crucial stage. These children need the space to move freely and spontaneously, to learn to control their bodies (Cleave and Brown 1991). Good use needs to be made of the outside area so children can work 'on a larger, more active scale than is possible indoors' (QCA 2000, p. 15). Outdoors seems the most natural place to ensure children have plenty of space. Even if the outdoor area is small the sheer 'feel' of being outside makes it seem larger. Overcrowding can cause aggressive behaviour (Bates 1996). (See also Chapter 6.)

Furniture and resources

Outdoors, furniture and resources need to be provided. Furniture will include something to sit on, something to work at and something to store equipment in. Resources for a particular activity need to be close by and other equipment that children may want should be accessible. The resources chosen should enable children to work independently or in groups. The siting of equipment can affect play and may need repositioning if causing congestion points. Consideration needs to be given to whether resources are clearly labelled, tidy and aesthetically pleasing. There needs to be exploratory areas for scientific work. If the outside and inside are to be viewed in the same way then learning areas or bays are needed in the outdoor play space (see

Chapter 5). Indoors there may be a book corner, graphics area, technology table, paint area, building and construction section and so on, so that when the complete room is looked at, the whole curriculum is on offer around the room. Outdoors, the whole curriculum also needs to be seen to be available. Areas therefore need to be delineated for:

- design, building and construction,
- active and vigorous physical work,
- imaginative play,
- scientific discovery,
- language and mathematical work.

In this way, the curriculum is on offer across the whole area. Consideration can then be given to what activities might be moved from indoors to outdoors, such as painting. Space needs to be made available outside for quiet and reflective play, away from others.

Expectations

An important managerial issue to address is the expectations of the staff, and this has to encompass regulations and rules; rules in the widest sense of the word, showing what is allowed and what is not. Class expectations have to be considered whatever the age of the children and intentions and structures must be conveyed to them (Moyles 1992, Wragg 1993). These expectations reflect the values of the staff and have to be made explicit to the children. It should also be possible to involve children in this process, so that they can feel that they have contributed to the rules. Without clear guidelines children and staff can feel vulnerable and unsure. Children may then not try things out for themselves as they do not know or are unsure whether this is the expectation of this particular class. This is an example of how the hidden curriculum can undermine the planned curriculum as described in Blenkin and Whitehead (1988). Looking to the ORACLE work, even though it is not concerned with nursery-aged children, may provide some relevant findings (Galton *et al.* 1980). Here the pupils were found to want to please the teacher and do what she wanted and they tried to avoid high-risk situations, which might put them in a vulnerable situation. The conclusion from the study is that teachers need to demonstrate clearly what it is they want and value, otherwise children will not try out new and high-risk situations. For example, if independent thought and learning is wanted, this has to be clearly demonstrated. Rules cannot be 'set in stone' and their implications have to be thought through. Otherwise the rules will not be working for the good of the children; expectations are there for the children's benefit and not to hinder play.

   Expectations will include such issues as how children:

- can approach their play,
- be helped in their play,
- be helped to continue their play.

Consideration needs to be given to how children are encouraged to think through problems themselves, or whether staff are seen as the fount of all knowledge. Are children allowed to move indoor equipment outside or not? Can children move their play from one area to the another?

   If children are unable to do such things then it is highly unlikely that they can follow through particular interests and concerns and so this will affect how they approach independent learning. Do staff work at all activities or concentrate on a few, thereby giving high status to some activities and low status to others? The way the classroom is organised for learning and the way it is handled on a daily basis will affect how children think and find out. Gura (1992) argues that how we organise time and space affects how children feel about themselves and others. Social awareness, social understanding and personal autonomy will be dictated by the way the class is organised and managed (Blenkin and Whitehead 1988). The guidance makes a clear connection between the organisation of the environment and attitudes to learning; positive attitudes coming from rich and stimulating experiences, such as resources which inspire and encourage children to initiate thier own learning (QCA 2000, p. 14).

Practical issues

There are many issues of a practical nature which need to be considered before children can enter the early years garden. Unlike indoors, the weather will have an effect on the outdoor area. Issues will include clothing and footwear and how the outdoors may affect some equipment. It is more effective to respond to each day as it comes, rather than having blanket rules, such as 'no going on the grass from September to March'. In a sense, the outdoors has to be inspected in the same way as a cricket pitch before a match. It may be cold and damp, and the grass may be very muddy and staff will decide that for a couple of days children will not go on the grass as it is simply too slippery. Children can be part of such discussions and may come up with solutions not thought of by the staff. A week later it may still be damp and cold but the grass may be not so bad and so Wellington boots can be decided on. It is not a necessary or sensible idea always to expect outdoor shoes, as this can radically affect the flow of play, but they may be necessary on occasions. In terms of issues such as gloves and coats, again you have to see what the weather is like. A box of spare gloves and boots will make sure that no child is denied access to the outdoors.

In conclusion

The three-year study of children learning in 19 randomly-arranged classrooms com-pared with 19 structured classrooms found that there were differences in learning outcomes and that spatial organisation did have an impact on learning (Nash 1981). The structured classrooms were those where attention had been paid to the issues under the heading of environment and the space was deliberately arranged to promote learning (p. 144). Children in the randomly-arranged class showed less evidence of development than children in the planned classrooms. Children in the randomly-arranged classrooms were often interrupted in their work and unable to move onto more complex tasks.

The Nash research also argues that spatial organisation does convey messages to children about what the teacher sees as important. If an adult is mostly involved with some art and craft activity, children will soon pick up that staff see this type of activity as more important than those that they do not spend much time with. Blenkin and Whitehead (1988) argue that if the environment is not considered and planned for, the effect of this can actually undermine what the teacher is proposing for children's learning in the first place. So the place in which we expect learning to take place has to reflect the learning we are expecting. By paying careful attention to the details of the working environment, by giving due consideration to space, time, ethos, approach, we can make it easier for children to learn by offering the most appropriate mode for learning. Offering tarmac and a few bikes for 26 children means that limited learning is anticipated. However, if we require children to converse and develop not only their language but ideas through talk, then we have to arrange that environment so that talk can be inspired. If we require children to be independent learners, then we have to provide an environment which they can affect and modify. We cannot then expect them to come and ask for various resources and materials as this undermines the independence we are trying to enhance. If we want children to learn to interact and consider others, then we have to provide situations where they can play and work in groups. If children cannot mix and match resources we undermine their ability to make connections in their learning.

It may be that the physical space is not the best we could have hoped for and not the most perfectly designed, but it still has to be considered and planned for, so that it becomes a worthwhile learning and teaching space. Through our attention to the environment we can, it would seem, either help or hinder learning. And should we not be in this profession to make learning easy and accessible?

Management and organisation are at the heart of our work; they 'make or break' us. Wragg (1993) argues that the most imaginative teacher will fail if organisation and management have not been addressed. This holds true for any teaching and learning setting whether it be under a ceiling or beneath the clouds.

2: A combined environment

> Outdoor activity should be seen as an integral part of early years provision and ideally should be available to children all the time. The adults planning for the class should be thinking about the indoor and outdoor areas not as separate spaces but as linked areas where a child involved in an activity may move between them, using the equipment and resources which best meet her or his needs where and when the play requires them. (Lasenby 1990, p. 5)

Probably the single most important issue to address is *when* outdoor play is available. Lasenby (1990), McLean (1991), Lally and Hurst (1992), Dowling (1992), Gura (1992), Bilton (1993), Robson (1996), QCA (2000) all clearly argue for the combined indoor and outdoor environment. In fact, problems are created both indoors and outdoors if outdoor play is offered on a timetable basis (Bilton 1993). By offering both simultaneously and as one, both will work well. By offering outdoor play alongside indoor play you are acknowledging that outdoor play is as important and as relevant to young children's learning. By offering it simultaneously it naturally becomes an equal partner in the planning process and both areas can complement each other.

Difficulties with timetabled outdoor play

A graphic effect of the timetabled outdoor play session can be seen indoors. The Gura (1992) research into block play found that children would abandon play activities inside so that they could get outside first. The play these children were involved in was high quality and offered them interest; they were therefore actively engaged. However, the pull of outside was too strong and the timetabled outdoor play actually caused much of the learning inside to abruptly stop. In this study, children would see others rushing to get outside – often it was those children who had had less to clear away – and in their frustration the children left behind would simply not complete their job and slip outside. Gura argues that the fragmentation of the day, where outdoor play was timetabled, created a 'hit and run' approach to play (p. 184). Personal experience back this up: in one nursery, even though the activities available outdoors were very limited, children would abandon a snack to get outside and stay there for as long as possible. Children may abandon what they are doing indoors to get outdoors, whether the outdoor play area is well or poorly resourced, simply because the pull of a new area is too much for them.

The impact of timetabled outdoor play can affect the play outside too. Here, if all the children are expected to go outside there is the prospect of too many children trying to access too little equipment and too few resources. But this can also happen when children have a choice of indoors or outdoors during a timetabled outdoor play session, as often initially, most children will rush outside. Wherever the learning environment, it does take children time to settle. When children first enter the early years setting they will take differing times to settle down to concentrated work. They may at first go to one activity but this may be through habit and for security, they may then move on to take up their preferred, first, sustained activity or it may take some time before they settle. Where the outdoor play is timetabled, children will move outside at the designated time, but will need a period of readjustment before they select their preferred activity. It could be that for some children this will take all the time they have outside and, just as they are about to settle, it is time to move inside again.

Bruce (1987) suggests that, by limiting experiences, for example using the climbing frame only once a week, 'skills are not encouraged and accidents are more likely' (p. 59). We all know what it is like to start something, then to be interrupted, go back to it saying: 'now where was I?' We have to retread old ground just to pick up where we left off. Not only is this very dull, it is also very frustrating. Children will experience this if equipment is only available periodically or for very short periods. They will get used to the equipment or resource, but find that just as they are about to learn something new it is put away. The next week comes round, they start getting used to the equipment again and the same thing happens. They will spend most of the time revisiting, rather than learning anything new, and in fact their skill acquisition may regress. Cullen (1993), looking at children's use and perceptions of outdoor play in New Zealand, came to similar conclusions. She argues that children may not reach the levels of confidence or skills expected, simply because they are not in the outdoor area for long enough.

Timetabling outside play can create a situation where staff see this time as the same as the primary playtime, when staff have a break, and a drink, when indoors can be cleared away. Timetabling can mean that staff feel disinclined to put much effort or thought into what is on offer to children and what learning is achieved. Cullen (1993) found that the longer the outdoor play period the better the quality of play, especially creative play, and that the more complex forms of cooperative play were facilitated by the staff. She concludes that the reason for this is simple. The longer the children spent outside the more the staff had to plan for. The more staff had to plan for, the more effort they put into the plans and so the more interesting the range of activities. This would seem to make a great deal of sense. When children are outdoors for a short period of time, faced with a few toys to play with, staff may have to spend most of this time sorting out conflicts between children. These conflicts can be difficult to resolve as the resources are not available to help children to move onto some other worthwhile play. So, in these circumstances the very timetabling of outdoor play creates a host of problems, which would not have been there if outdoor play had been available alongside indoor play. In this climate, it is a case of the survival of the fittest, with some children unwilling to go outside as they are too frightened and others staying very close to the adult, almost for protection.

Although a study of primary playtime, the findings by Blatchford (1989) are quite relevant to the early years setting if outdoor play is treated in the same way as primary playtime. In this study it was found that:

- many children were scared to go out at playtime,
- behaviour was often poor,
- children got bored with little to occupy them, and
- many hung around the supervising adult.

Primary playtime was designed to enable children to have fresh air and some exercise after the sedentary activities of the day: a far cry from an effective teaching and learning environment.

Where there is little to do and very little interaction with adults, and no quality high level interactions, certain groups of children can become dominant, for example, boys, older children or the more aggressive. Behaviour can also become static with children doing the same things whether they want to or not, because they have been channelled and no one is helping to challenge this. It could be argued that this stereotypical play is innate, but there is no research evidence either way. In any case it means that groups of children could be being denied access to something which may be of use to them in their learning.

Timetabling can also send very clear messages to children about how staff view outdoor play. By offering it for a short time and with little or no planning, children, staff and parents will see it as somewhere less important than indoors. This in itself can create problems in that children are more likely to demonstrate non-purposeful behaviour and not settle to anything, as it is not expected. Lally and Hurst (1992) suggest that having a set playtime can encourage the staff to see outdoor play simply in terms of physical development (p. 86). The timetabling stops staff seeing the outdoor area as an extension to the classroom and all that that entails, with a whole curriculum on offer. So, during the timetabled slot children will be running around, playing with balls and riding bikes. It therefore follows that staff, children and parents will then view physical activity as less important than anything which goes on in the classroom. The logic is that if schools only provide something for fifteen minutes a day then it must be less important than other activities which are provided for much longer.

Having time to play and work

Interestingly enough, in Paley's (1984) study of children's behaviour in her class, she found that when she increased the amount of free playtime, and spread it out over a longer period, the boys ventured to the table activities to do more work-orientated activities, rather than continue to play. Her conclusions from this observation were that the children had been given sufficient time to play and fantasise, the play had not been packed into a frantic time and so the children were happy to move on to more school-orientated activities. Children had been able to go between play and activities in the knowledge that the free play was not to be taken away. The girls actually played imaginatively more than they had previously, but, given that they tended to do more of the work activities, they did not suffer in the school setting or in school tests.

These findings are borne out by a study into changing a nursery routine from including a short timetabled outdoor playtime, to making indoors and outdoors available simultaneously (Bilton 1993). In the class in the study, outdoor play was timetabled, midway through the session, for fifteen minutes. All the children were expected to go outside. Prior to the change, when children went outside their behaviour was manic, they rushed around with little or no purpose to their play. They were in essence doing what was expected, that is, 'letting off steam'. When the change was made and indoors and outdoors became available simultaneously, all of the children dashed outside to play the moment the outside door was opened. The staff concluded that the children thought outdoor play would be taken away from them, therefore they needed to get out as soon as possible. It was also concluded that the children thought that it would only be open for a very short period of time as it had been previously. As the experiment progressed and out and in continued to be available all the time and at the same time, this 'mad dash' stopped and children went out and in calmly whenever they wanted. In fact, it took three days for the children not to rush out immediately the door was open and to start making informed choices as to where they would play and when. The staff found that when indoors and outdoors were available for the whole session, the play outside was much more sustained and effective and the previous manic behaviour simply ceased. Indeed, the staff were surprised at just how much the children's behaviour changed in such a short period.

There was a clear connection between organisation and behaviour. The short, timetabled, compulsory outdoor play session caused the non-purposeful behaviour, while the planned, full session, combined indoor and outdoor learning and teaching environment created informed and concentrated play. Again, the findings of Cullen (1993) are borne out by this research, in that the longer outdoor play period meant the staff wanted to, and did, plan for the area and considered how the two areas could work to support each other. This is a clear example of where problems associated with outdoor play were completely and easily surmountable.

The above findings are also given weight and support by the Cleave and Brown (1991) study into four-year-olds in infant classes. This clearly argues for children to be given time to pursue interests and have blocks of uninterrupted play. The authors cite research by Barrett (1986) which recommends that time needs to be given to children so that they can think, reflect, consolidate and master what they are learning. Stevenson (1987) argues that, when children are given time to work at an activity, they can concentrate for a considerable period of time and the children in her study did so. But, to concentrate and persevere, children need to know that the time is available to do so. Lally (1991) argues that 'a whole class approach is clearly not consistent with a developmental approach where individual needs are of paramount concern' (p. 78). Children cannot be approached as individuals or learn as individuals if the routine of the nursery involves interruptions and blocks of time devoted to whole-group activities, such as all going out to play.

Dispelling the myths

A number of difficulties can be raised by teachers as to why outdoors and indoors cannot be provided simultaneously throughout the session. These include the weather, supervision, lack of space and setting up. Unlike the indoor class, the outdoor class is affected by the weather; however, the most common climatic condition which affects the use of the outdoors, is rain. The advantage of having both indoors and outdoors freely available for the entire session is that the weather can be worked round. When outdoor play is at a specific time of day everyday, children cannot go out if it then rains. However, if outdoors is available throughout the session children can go out when it is not raining, and utilise the best of the weather, whatever time of the day. Obviously, staff have to tune into the weather forecasts and be confident about the day's weather, so they do not set up the equipment only to find five minutes later that it is raining heavily.

The day-to-day study of the weather can prove to be a highly effective learning tool for the children and can bring in all kinds of learning, including the skills of observation and prediction. Some staff will argue that it can be too cold for children to go out, but there will be very few days when it is so cold that children cannot go outside. But for the rest of the time if children are wrapped up well, and have enough to play with they will not get cold. When staff play with children and are as active as them they also find they do not get cold. Classes need to be prepared for all types of weather and have boxes of spare gloves, hats, scarves, boots, shoes, and for summer long-sleeved tee-shirts and hats. Having these available means the move from indoors to outdoors can be as easy as possible.

Figure 2.1 An example of combining play inside with play out. The post office was inside and the parcel office outside.

Some staff argue that the supervision of two areas is difficult when there are only two members of staff. If both areas have been planned carefully, there are not too many activities on offer in either, and therefore sufficient activities which children can use with or without adult involvement, then one adult indoors and one outdoors is possible. Many children frantically accessing a climbing frame does give cause for concern with regard to safety. And when staff raise concerns about using both areas simultaneously this is the sort of picture they usually have. However, this particular scenario will not arise if outdoors and indoors are planned thoughtfully and thoroughly. Many classes do indeed have students, and, of course, parental helpers. Equally, staff need to make sure that, wherever they are, they are scanning the area to make sure children are settled, to pre-empt any possible conflicts and be aware of any dangerous situations. It is therefore not sufficient for staff to get involved in only one activity. Scanning, being abreast of all situations in the class (Kounin 1970, Pollard and Tann 1987) and moving gently into group settings are all instrumental in ensuring successful behaviour management.

With indoors and outdoors available at the same time staff also need to have a flexible rota so they can respond to the children's desire to move from one activity to the next, indoors or outdoors. In this way, if a member of staff is working with one group of children and they wish to move their play outside and the adult to stay with them, this can happen. The member of staff positioned outside can then move inside without any children having to be disturbed. Research by Bilton (1993) found that one member of staff outdoors and one indoors worked well as long as the scanning, moving about and flexible rota were adhered to.

Staff need to agree how to manage the situation if an accident occurs and there are only two members of staff available. All the children could be moved to one area, or one member of staff could move into a supervisory role keeping an eye on both areas, while the other member of staff dealt with the accident.

Some staff argue that the outdoor area is too small for it to be of much use and resort to using it on a fixed playtime basis. However, too many children, in too confined a space, can create problems such as aggressive and dangerous behaviour. But, if outdoors and indoors are provided together the small size of an outdoor area is not such a problem. If children have quality activities available both indoors and outdoors, it will only be on rare occasions that any activity will be oversubscribed, or that any area will be completely devoid of children. Even on summer days, children still like to spend time working inside and likewise on very cold days children want to spend time working outside. If children are following current interests and concerns this will dictate what they play with. A small outside space can in fact be made into a particularly cosy area by virtue of its size.

Some staff argue that setting up outside takes too long, but this does not have to take an inordinate amount of time, nor should it be too strenuous. Again, if planned carefully, sufficient activities are made available and there is a good range to cover imaginative, constructional as well as physical play, then setting up will flow easily. Putting out fifteen bikes and a slide can seem quite arduous, but this is not an arrangement which would be expected in a carefully planned and resourced garden. Staff who have indoors and outdoors running as integral environments and who plan the two as one, find that setting up is not arduous but very stimulating as they are always thinking of new ways to interest and entice the children.

Unattached outdoor area

There are some settings where the outdoor play area is not just outside the classroom, is not attached to the classroom, but is in fact set away from the room. Quite clearly this is not an ideal situation. If the situation can be changed so the outdoor area is attached to the classroom this should be done. However, if this is not possible then adaptations to usual practice will have to be made. The difficulty perceived with this situation is that children cannot move freely between the two areas, and it is not appropriate to allow under-fives to wander from the class through an unfenced area to the garden. One answer is a secure pathway, with fencing on either side so that children can only move between the two areas without going astray. A path such as this may cut across a primary playground, but could be opened at certain spots so infant children can access their whole playground. When the primary children are having their playtime, it may be that the free access between the class and outdoor play area would not be possible. However, still working on the premise that outdoors and indoors are a combined and integral environment and that the two areas should be available at all times, you would need to have one staff member indoors and one outdoors and one 'floating'. The children would have to opt for where they would start playing and then if they wished to move would need to be escorted. Or it may have to be organised so the 'floating' member of staff would move back and forth with children say every ten to fifteen minutes. It is a case of trial and error in the setting and, once agreed with the children, they will fit in with the system admirably, although there may be teething problems as there usually are when starting any new system.

It will also be necessary to make sure that the complete curriculum is on offer in both areas, so that writing, reading and mathematical activities are covered. Having a split between indoors and outdoors does make life more difficult, but the difficulties caused by having a timetabled playtime are far greater than those created by having outdoors and indoors available simultaneously.

Structure of the day

Wherever the children are being educated, the format of the day would be similar. Children and parents will need a period of time at the beginning of the session when they can talk to the staff. After that both out and in can be freely available, but the opening of outdoors should never be announced, as this can disturb all children and their concentrated play and work. Both areas need to be open together for as long as possible but definitely not less an hour, as this gives children time to develop their ideas and learn and for staff to give necessary input. The free play period needs to be at the beginning of the session, rather than at the end. Otherwise it will be seen simply as a treat and holding little value educationally – 'you can follow your interests when you've done the important work with me'.

After that time there can be whole group work, for those children for whom it is appropriate. This might be a language or mathematics session, music, movement, PE. Then children can tidy up and there may be a story time to finish the session or group discussion. Whatever, the amount of time outside one needs to:

plan activities outside;
plan adult involvement;
look at the children's needs;
plan activities which join play inside and out;
provide resources;
make observations;
compensate for the constraints and exploit the opportunities of the environment.

If the children are at school all day then the afternoon format will be similar to the morning. It is better if young children (who may be as young as 48 months) do not have to be part of the whole school for lunch and playtime. However, this may be unavoidable, in which case giving them toys to play with (as in case study 1 below) and having closer adult support would be helpful. It may be possible for these children to use the Foundation Stage outdoor area at lunchtime.

Infant outdoor provision

Children are supposed to start formal education after their fifth birthday, but over the years there have always been under-fives in statutory school. The plight of four and sometimes three-year-olds in school has been of concern. For example in the late 1980s the NFER research project looking into four-year-olds in school was begun (Cleave and Brown 1991), highlighting the inappropriateness of both the content and approach of the education on offer in many school settings. With the desirable learning outcomes the concern was still there but little was done to help.

The Foundation Stage is now trying to ensure that wherever the under-five is being educated, the content and approach is right for the age and stage. Making changes to practice in nursery classes and schools has limited impact as these settings are tending to follow educational processes close to the Foundation Stage guidance already. However, in the infant/primary sector the impact has been much greater. Prior to the Foundation Stage reception children were following the National Curriculum plus in most schools the literacy and numeracy hours. This has now changed and children are expected to experience a more traditional nursery curriculum. One of the greatest changes having to be made to practice, is in regard to outdoor play.

Current thinking considers it is more effective to actually educate all the children under five as a group within a Foundation Stage unit, rather than having reception and year 1 and 2 mixed. Some schools have in fact made the nursery into a nursery unit, incorporating all the reception children. Otherwise the National Curriculum will always be the dominant curriculum and to run both a Foundation Stage and National Curriculum is a lot of work for staff. However, in some schools, usually rural, there are insufficient children for separate classes and so children will be educated together in one class. Time will have to be spent making sure the children do have a movement-orientated curriculum though. It is also important to feel secure in the knowledge that outdoor play is not going to do the over-fives any damage! It is perfectly permissible for over-fives to use the outdoor area as well as the under-fives; there is no dictate that states 'no over-five should use the outdoor area'. In fact everyone needs periods away from intense work, and play can simply be a time to let the brain go at a less intense rate. Children and adults are much more successful if they do have periods of time away from the 'work'. A Reception/Year 1 and 2 class visited had activities available outside all the time. The Foundation Stage children were able to free flow the two areas, the KS1 children were able to use outside but on a rotational basis, five at a time. These children had a number of activities they had to do each day and marked these off as they did them and one of the activities was to work outside. However, they had to make sure they completed the 'work' activities for that day. In other words they couldn't play, outside all the time and forget the work. There was a very restful atmosphere in the class, and no undirected behaviour – children could relax through play, not by being 'silly' in the corner with a friend.

How, then, can this be organised? It is necessary to return to the guiding principles in the Introduction to answer this. Firstly, there has to be a belief in outdoor play. Secondly, as far as possible both environments have to work simultaneously. Otherwise, all the problems previously mentioned will occur. Therefore the space available does need to be just outside the classroom. Ideally the space needs to be fenced. If this is not possible, it may be necessary to create some kind of boundary in the form of a chalk line, or a foldaway fence, or with the expedient placing of furniture to be used in this area. Through discussions and periodic reviews with the children there should be few difficulties with their behaviour. Thirdly, the area needs to be well thought out and planned alongside indoor play and in such a way that it is not seen as an area to play in once the work has been done, but as part and parcel of the whole teaching and learning setting. Otherwise, as has already been argued, this will create behavioural problems.

It may be that only a part of the curriculum can be offered in this area. So, for example, it may not be possible to offer a climbing component in the area, but there can still be some physical activity on offer, perhaps skipping or ball skills. It may be that the area has to be structured so that it is only for a limited number of children at a time, and on offer on a rotational basis, as part of one of the activities on offer for that day. It may in fact be possible to house two or three activities at a time.

The outdoor area that can be used very effectively for imaginative play, as it gives children space. So this area could be devoted to imaginative activities with its own resources box and equipment, with children also being able to access indoor equipment (see Chapter 5 for a resource list).

It is essential to work alongside children in the area, observe how the children are getting on and assess their learning. In the Cleave and Brown (1991) study the researcher's presence outside actually encouraged children to move there, whereas beforehand when there was no adult outside children did not move out of doors (p. 131). If there is extra help in the class, whether nursery nurses, teaching assistants or parents, then all the adults can assist in supporting all areas of activity. However, an adult based continually in the outdoor area, particularly if this is a small space, may not be a good idea as this may inhibit some children. This cannot be a complete outdoor learning area, but what is provided should depend on the needs of the children.

One has to bear in mind that some children may feel more settled in this environment than others and so the more formal work could (and in this case, should) be incorporated into the imaginative play outside. It may be that some children prefer to read and write outside and get better results if they do. In the Cleave and Brown study (1991) one child who was unsure and passive indoors during the morning session was an active, interested child outside in the afternoon. The authors argue that this may in part be because of the greater range of activities available outside, but could also have been because of the placing of resources in the outdoor environment (pp. 131–2). In this study, space, positioning and choice of activities revealed different aspects of the child, demonstrating the impact of how we provide the learning and teaching environment (pp. 131–2.). Outside can also be an area where children can work quietly. Quiet corners can be very difficult to find in a classroom.

In terms of time management it is not appropriate to offer an hour of literacy and an hour of maths in the morning. The Foundation Stage guidance talks in terms of literacy and numeracy being offered across the day rather than as a single unit (QCA 2000, p. 27). If the principles of the guidance are followed, then it is wholly inappropriate for under-fives to receive two hours of literacy and numeracy everyday. These subjects can be offered as a whole group activity but only for a short period of time. Both subjects will be occurring through the play, for example in imaginative play if children are writing up a menu, this is literacy. If children are talking, this is literacy. If children are throwing balls at named numbers, this is mathematics. However, staff will need to show through planning and assessment, the elements of literacy and numeracy within these child-initiated and child-orientated activities. Most classes have a focused activity everyday and within this there will be elements of numeracy and literacy. Story time can be awash with literacy.

Where the head teacher and other staff are supportive of, and committed to, outdoor play, changes can be made so that four-year-olds in a reception class can have access to the outdoors. Moving the four-year-olds to a class that has access to outside, putting in or re-siting doors so that outside can be accessed, are two possible solutions. Making changes to the whole school timetable so that children can be given time outside and/or free choice of outdoors and indoors is another. Looking at the overall staffing, so that children and a staff member can play and work outside (Cleave and Brown 1991) is yet another. Long term, schools could look ahead to raising funds for a covered area, a fenced area, raised garden beds or for hard surfaces for use with building and construction activities and wheeled toys.

Whatever changes are made one cannot expect it to work overnight. It is so easy to make changes that do not go as had been expected on the first day and then to give up. For example, in the study, changing from a set outdoor time to it being available simultaneously with indoors, it took the children three days to start thinking about where they wished to play, as opposed to rushing out the moment the doors opened (Bilton 1993). I recently had a conversation with a teacher who had changed the snack time from a whole group activity to self-service, so children could choose when to drink and eat. On the first day all the children chose to have the snack first thing, so there were 26 children sitting round the self-service table! Staff against the new set up, were quick to say 'there, told you it wouldn't work'. But the teacher gave it a few days and of course children soon understood what the new system was about and got their snack when they were ready to. When making changes think about what one can manage and what is measurable. In this way one can see if the changes have had a positive effect. Finally, be prepared to make necessary adjustments.

Hertfordshire LEA have just begun an outdoor curriculum project. Twelve schools have been accepted onto the project to make changes to their outdoor provision. The project will last for eight months and schools have put together a range of proposals to develop their outdoor provision. Much of the work concerns the reception classes. Ideas include actually changing the outdoor environment, buying suitable resources, combining three reception classes, planning, information to parents, reviewing the link between the Foundation Stage and Key Stage 1, monitoring, writing a policy on play, improving the quality of learning through play, covering the areas of learning outside and combining reception and year 1. This is an exciting project and one which merits success. Time has been given over to making changes and schools are being supported by the authority. The project gives outdoor provision a high level of credibility.

Case studies

To make the above suggestions come alive it would seem useful to actually discuss how some teachers in infant classes have interpreted the Foundation Stage guidance, within the confines of their own setting, with regard to outdoor play. All of the schools and staff are at different points in their understanding of outdoor play and in the provision. The staff range from having had nursery training to not having any, from being in teaching many years to only being in post for two years. None of these teachers would say they are offering perfect outdoor provision and play; all would like to do more outside. They are all having a go, all see the potential of the outdoor learning environment and see it as an ongoing project.

Case study 1

Infant school
Reception class
60 children
4 members of staff – 2 teachers, 2 teaching assistants.
2 class bases, 4 areas of learning – construction, creative, investigative, quiet.

2 outside areas – playground not attached to the class, includes grass, tree and slope to hedge. Inner courtyard accessible from classroom through creative learning area, includes decking, paving and a fixed sandpit. The two areas lend themselves to different learning – the front playground being an area for the development of physical skills, horticulture, investigation and the inner courtyard for investigation and construction. The inner courtyard was considered easier to 'supervise' and not in need of constant adult presence. The inner courtyard was originally just a dead space and has been designed and changed to create a proper teaching and learning area.

In the morning the children have a half hour time in the playground from 10.30–11am. Everyone goes out and the focus is on gross motor, role-play, music and art. The activities are taken out and set up 15 minutes before the actual play session and linked to work being done inside. Three members of staff work with the children at any one time, two of these directly working with the children – 'facilitating' – and the third making observations of identified children.

At lunchtime these children follow the usual lunchtime procedures, but the staff do like to leave some activities outside for all children to use, including years 1 and 2.

The afternoon period is run slightly differently to the morning and the children can choose which of the four areas of learning they would like to work in and can move from one to another. Through a study of the children and discussions with staff, independence, an aspect of enthusiasm, was seen as a crucial component of the personal and social education. Outside was seen as the best environment to allow independence to be fostered through play, by having resources freely available, time to interact, and where an ethos that said independence was 'okay'. Associated with the creative learning area are activities set up outside in the inner courtyard. Activities may include easels, role-play, water tray, sandpit, books, music, in fact just about anything can be set up in this area, except gross motor as the space available is not big enough. This free period is run between 1.30 and 2.30pm.

The children go out 'whatever the weather'. The teacher felt it was important to involve all in the changes to practice and particularly parents, who want to understand why schools do things as they do. Outdoor play was considered a success, as children showed their 'real selves'. In this well planned and managed environment children are able to really play, are enthusiastic, do not view the time as 'work' and staff have time to observe children in this 'true state'.

The teacher is now with year 1s and is introducing outdoor play, as she feels children need this freedom, this chance to be successful with others, this time to be in a place they enjoy, but which unfortunately they are so often denied when at home. Children have the opportunity to work and play outside once a week, either for a half morning or afternoon session and then during choosing time two times a week. The teacher feels this experience enhances learning and children's social and emotional development.

Case study 2

> Large rural primary school
> Reception/Year 1 class
> 29 children
> 1 teacher and 1 teaching assistant

The classroom is in a terrapin building housing the FS/Year 1 children and a Year 2 class. The outdoor space is L-shaped and prior to the changes simply a walkway, a dead space.

Fences were installed either end of the space. The teacher then transformed this space by adding various areas for learning. She made four sensory areas – shiny things such as a collection of CDs and mirrors for sight, chimes for hearing, scented flowers and herbs for smell and coloured stones, pebbles and bark for touch. These areas are distinct from one another and create a sense of peace and quiet.

The teacher has developed a vegetable plot, which at present has beans growing started from seed inside, purple sprouting broccoli, leeks, carrots, strawberry plants and an archway with sweet peas.

The nature area is wild and has a log and old carpet for the encouragement of minibeasts. Plus there is scientific equipment such as rain gauges.

Tree stumps create a seating area and children often take glove puppets out to run self-organised mini drama sessions.

In another space there is an abacus and 100 square, plus blackboards.

A small sandpit, with a Perspex lid has recently been added. And children can sit on cushions to play at the sandpit. A low level shed has been purchased to house the larger items, such as trikes, wooden train set, road signs, balancing blocks and of course gardening and sand equipment.

Although this beautification was not a necessity, it did actually change the nature of the area from a walkway to a working environment and gave it a high level of credibility. The teacher estimated the cost was around £250–£350, she used shops such as IKEA to make purchases and did co-opt the help of a boyfriend and father!

In the morning the outdoor area is used to support the work of literacy or numeracy with the younger children and those who need more hands on experiences to help with their understanding. The teacher always makes sure the children who have been working outside share their findings and show any work to the rest of the class – for example writing patterns in the sand, flower designs and mathematical sums from pebbles.

In the afternoon it can be that the whole class is outside, for example working at some aspect of science. Recently the topic of plants has been taught and children were set the task of finding various plant types – not green, smelling, feathery leaves and so on; working at a differentiation by outcome level. Interestingly enough the boys spent longer on this task outside than they would have on a task inside, they communicated more with the teacher than usual and with each other on the subject.

On a Friday there is 'golden time' when children have the opportunity to choose their own activities. Children may choose to work inside or out, but have to set up and put away whatever they choose to play with. This may include painting, construction, small world, role play. The teacher has found that four chairs with a piece of material draped over the top to make a den is a very successful and popular activity and more popular than the bought pop-up tent.

The teacher found the addition of the outdoor area a bonus; it meant the small classroom was no longer always overcrowded and cramped. She found that the children were happy to play outside and were happy in themselves; she found that some children learnt more easily outside and she would not want to return to not having an outside area. In fact the children clearly see it as a significant learning area – they recently noticed an old silver bucket which had been thrown out and suggested planting it up with lovely polyanthus.

The outdoor area is rougly rectangular, with a grassed slope in the middle, on which there are two tress and a stone path down the least steep part of the slope. At the bottom of the slope is a tarmac path. At the top of the slope the ground levels off and consists of tarmac and grass, on which there is a permanent sandpit and wooden house.

Importantly, the teacher is enabling the children to use outside, is providing activities, clearly values the area and so enables the children to do so. There was little equipment specific to outside, but the teacher is building up her stock. This teacher saw the outdoor environment as an ongoing project and one that would need looking at constantly.

Case study 3

Primary school
60 children
2 teachers and the equivalent of 2½ teaching assistants
2 class bases

This school is in the process of transforming its Foundtion Stage unit. They have created a reasonable sized fenced outdoor area, with a 10 x 13 metre rectangular safety surface set in the middle of this area.

The cost was around £9,000 and included new fencing, the re-laying of slabs, the laying of the safety surface, the flattening of one corner where a pond had been and the installation of gates. Half the money was raised by the PTA, half was donated by the governing body.

The staff are in the midst of trying out and changing practice, at the moment the children go out for around an hour in the morning and in the afternoon as it fits in. The play is somewhat free and staff are trying to get to grips with what quality play is all about.

This school has made a commitment to the Foundation Stage and in particular outdoor play within the Stage. They do not have all the answers, and are grappling with ideas not known to all of them. What is important is that they are giving it a go, they are willing to try, and accept that practice and provision are not going to be transformed overnight.

Case study 4

Infant school
Rising-fives class – five mornings per week.
19–24 children
2 members of staff – 1 teacher and 1 teaching assistant

The nursery class garden is used by the rising-fives class, reception class and nursery class. Therefore the rising-fives and reception classes have to walk to the area.

The children go into the nursery class outdoor area for half an hour. Therefore, all the children have to be escorted to this area and then have to use it together. The teacher either sets up the area before the children arrived or with the children.

The three classes within the Foundation Stage unit plan together and at present are using a grid system to note down activities that will be on offer each day.

Activities include:

Table top/bench tables – for construction, small world, art work.

Fixed wooden house for role-play, which is changed regularly, and well stocked with resources. For example, a flower shop (lots of goodies bought from the Pound shop), a railway station waiting room, a fairy tale castle. The last was resourced with cloaks (made from old curtains), a hobbyhorse, treasure chests (with jewels and treasure made from foil), crowns and scarves. All these resources are made and collected together for the sole use of outside play.

Wheeled toys – available only on Mondays and Wednesdays.

Tuesdays and Thursdays are for other gross motor activities. These include a selection of balls, basketball net, pop-up goal, home-made skittles. Sometimes children are given clipboards and score sheets to note their successes! Obstacle courses are regularly set up using carpet squares, drainpipes, crates, boxes, netting, drapes. Children use this area for imaginative and construction work, such as making dens, building sites and booby traps.

There is a fixed sandpit, which is given a focus each day.

On Fridays children are able to choose what activities they would like to use. Interestingly enough at the beginning of the term some children would choose the wheeled toys, but as the term progresses they were not so interested in choosing the wheeled toys. The conclusion drawn from this is that the children have so much else to choose from that the bikes held less interest.

Plants are grown at appropriate times during the year and scientific work tends to follow particular interests, such as rescuing worms as a consequence of too much rain – an equivalent of 'pet-rescue', renamed 'worm-rescue'!

The teacher was nursery trained and has many years of nursery experience. She felt she was not offering best quality outdoor play, but was doing the best she could in the circumstances. Behaviour was good and learning was happening. This was the result of careful planning, resourcing of activities, and adult involvement with children. The teacher would like to have a minimum of one hour outside everyday.

In the near future the area outside the reception and rising-fives classes will be fenced and joined with the nursery garden to make one large outdoor area, accessed by all three classes; working towards making a complete Foundation Stage unit.

In conclusion

For outdoor play to work well it has to be provided alongside indoor play. Both areas need to be seen, not as separate entities, but as combined, integral and complementary. It is apparent that many of the problems aired about outdoor play, including the problematic behaviour of children, the disturbance to indoor play, seeing outdoor play only in terms of physical play, are actually caused by having a fixed time for outdoor play. Having outdoors and indoors available at all times means that the problems associated with staffing, resourcing, the weather, children's behaviour are either removed or diminished. Timetabling outdoor play pays lip-service to it and can be of little use to children in their learning and development.

3: The outdoor environment – an historical perspective

I have always been intrigued by the fact that nursery schools and classes have an outdoor play area. It does not matter in what part of the country, whether a large or small class, nursery classes and schools will nearly always have this secure, outside, accessible area attached. The question is why? Where nursery classes are attached to primary schools, why isn't the infant playground used, maybe at a different time? The answer could be that under-fives need the security of a fenced area, not being old enough to play in an unfenced area, as they could wander off and they may be too unsure to play with older children. Perhaps parents need the security of knowing the children are able to play in a separate but secure area. Although these answers do so partly, they do not fully explain why this area exists. Static and movable toys and equipment are provided in this outdoor area and there are different surfaces, trees and shrubs. Staff are expected to work and play with children in this area as the space is open for the whole session.

This outdoor area is not unique to British nursery education. The United States, Australia and New Zealand, provide this outdoor area in their preschool centres and resource it in a similar way to the British nursery garden. So why is it that this strand of education differs from other spheres of education and particularly primary education? Why does this outdoor environment exist within the nursery? In this chapter I intend to look at the various influences that have played a part.

Influences

The answer appears to lie with origins. Looking back to the beginnings of nursery education in England, at the start of the nineteenth century, it is clear that the influences on it were different from those of any other sphere of education. Nursery education had very different roots from primary education and followed a different path. In part, nursery education grew from a dissatisfaction with the elementary education system and came about as a direct reaction to this schooling. Here children were not seen as individuals with particular needs, but were almost not seen, and they were expected to take what was offered, without comment. This was a harsh regime where children of three could be locked in a cupboard for daring to speak. The pioneers of nursery education viewed childhood and people's lives in different ways from those who ran compulsory elementary education. Their philosophy was formed from a number of differing influences which led to features unique to nursery education, which have come to be known as the 'common law' (Webb 1974) or 'the nursery tradition' (Pound 1987).

Nursery education, therefore, grew as a reaction to the poor and inappropriate quality of elementary education and was never a watered-down primary education. Likewise, outdoor play, which became a feature unique to nursery education, was a reaction to this inappropriate elementary education and was most definitely not a copy of primary playtime. In fact the garden was central to nursery education; it was the *raison d'être*. It is necessary to know about roots and influences to appreciate what outdoor play is and is not. Once understood it is much easier to organise.

Under-fives in elementary schools

Compulsory education came onto the statute book in 1870 and all children over the age of five had to go to school. Interestingly, the actual age of five was not chosen for sound psychological or social reasons but rather to enable MPs to wind up the business of the day in the House of Commons and so go home! (Szreter 1964). In the poorer families, children who had previously looked after their younger brothers and sisters found themselves compelled to go to school. Many of the younger siblings now found they had no one to look after them. Parents were either unwilling or unable to do so because they were working, childhood not being seen as something special. And so they were left at home or on the street. With nothing to do, these children started to drift into the schools to join their brothers and sisters. These young children, therefore, started to received an education which was geared to much older children, even though this was seen as inappropriate for the children it was supposed to be for. How much more inappropriate was it to the under-fives? Few schools attempted to gear the curriculum to suit these children's needs. Fifty to sixty children were expected to sit in tiered rows, for long periods, in cramped and often stuffy conditions. Children stayed all day at school; when they arrived they were already tired and hungry, and as school meals were not provided, stayed hungry. They were expected to stay still for long periods. They were expected to follow a very formal curriculum, to learn by rote, and were not to speak unless spoken to. Even the three-year-olds were expected to thread needles and do needlework. Matters were made worse because in some schools these children were then formally tested and, not surprisingly, many were found wanting.

By 1900 there were 43 per cent of children aged three to five attending elementary schools (Board of Education 1912). Such was the concern about the schooling that these young children were receiving that a report was commissioned to look into the conditions for the under-fives in schools. The Women Inspectors' Report on children under five years of age in public elementary schools makes for sad and alarming reading (Board of Education 1905). The Report considered that the elementary schools were wholly inappropriate for under-fives and that the work being given to them was harsh, too formal, too much time was devoted to the 3Rs, and the discipline was too rigid. The conditions were unhealthy; the classrooms were not well ventilated and the children were restricted in their movements. The Report speaks of babies being 'dulled' and the discipline being 'military' and concluded that children between three and five gained nothing by attending school (Board of Education 1905). So, overall, these under-fives were receiving an education not at all appropriate, and so, some would argue, were the over-fives. The reaction to the Report resulted in the exclusion of under-fives from school, placing them back on the streets, with all its dangers, with no one to care for them and with no solution to their plight in sight.

An interest in childhood

The children belonging to the poorest families lived in appalling conditions, where working hours were long and money scarce. Each family lived together in one room, each room in a house being occupied by another family. Children had disease-ridden bodies, infant mortality was high, malnutrition very evident. The Boer War and the First World War very clearly demonstrated the poor health of many citizens. There was a growing concern for the poorer sectors of society in both official and non-official circles and a desire for something to be done to help rectify the situation. There was a new interest in the health and welfare of everyone, but especially the young. There was a growing belief that many of the problems of ill-health and disease were in fact preventable.

There was also a growing concern for young children, with a changing attitude to the concept of childhood. Many began to see childhood as an important stage in life, with particular needs and requirements and so wanted to give it more significance than it had hitherto had (Steedman 1990). Children could not be treated as 'mini-adults' and seen as cheap labour as they had been in the past. After 1918 half-time education was phased out and all children had to go to school all day and so the worst excesses of child labour came to an end. The establishment of the psychological notion of stages of development, work on language acquisition and the detailed physiological accounts of physical growth all helped to view childhood as something which must be nurtured. Children came to be seen as the symbols of a better future for all.

The work of Friedrich Froebel (1782–1852) influenced those working with young children, and kindergartens were set up in poor areas of cities in the 1860s and 1870s and they became official Board of Education policy from 1890 onwards. The ideas of the nursery pioneers were linked to the changing view of man and society and the pioneers drew their ideas from Rousseau, Froebel, Pestalozzi, and Dewey. Margaret McMillan (1860–1931) was one of these nursery pioneers. She was influential in the nursery world and set up a nursery school in 1914, followed by a nursery training college. There were many others who set up nursery schools and also championed the cause of the poor, but her writings and talks made her stand out as particularly important in the nursery field. Through her work and political activities in Bradford and London she helped form Labour Party policy on childhood and the family. With other middle class women she devoted herself to the poor and to children (Steedman 1990). She, with other concerned citizens, felt that improving the health of poor children was paramount. Among her many achievements, she managed to ensure that subsidised school dinners became available in 1906 and in 1907 a schools medical inspections service was introduced.

The nursery garden

The nursery school evolved over time but it began with the setting up of outdoor camps in London. In 1911, Margaret McMillan, along with her sister Rachel, set up an outdoor camp for girls, aged 6 to 14, from the slum areas of Deptford. The children attended after school to have a bath, a meal and then to sleep outside. In the morning the children were given breakfast and then went to the Board school. The idea behind this experiment was to get the children out of the crowded, unhealthy conditions of their homes, in an attempt to improve their health, which it did dramatically. This work helped the sisters realise that outdoor living and the outdoor environment could have an impact on people's lives and help improve their health.

As a result of this work, the educational potential of working outside began to be seen. However, Margaret came to the conclusion that to have a lasting effect on these people's lives she needed to work with the youngest children. Hence her desire to set up a nursery school for children aged under five. She had come to realise that health and education went hand in hand, which was in direct conflict with elementary education, which was only concerned with education and did not see a link with health. She felt, for example, that if children had nasal problems this could lead to not being able to speak properly, sight problems could lead to not being able to read properly, lack of exercise could lead to deformity, tiredness to lack of interest.

All of this is now taken for granted. So a healthy body was considered necessary for a healthy mind. McMillan also came to the conclusion that the environment in which education was to take place had to be conducive to learning. The large, cramped, colourless environments of the elementary schools, where children sat and learned by rote, were not considered at all stimulating. Hence the desire to set up an interesting, enticing environment outside, where children could follow their interests.

The first nursery school was set up in Deptford in 1914, called the Rachel McMillan Open Air Nursery School. It started as an offshoot of the camps and began with six under-fives. The school started in the garden; the buildings or shelters (as they were named by McMillan) were erected to support the work within the garden. One could argue that the word 'school' was irrelevant, as this was associated with being inside a building; 'nursery garden education' may have been a better description of what she was trying to achieve. The buildings were there to act as a shelter in poor weather, to store equipment and to house washing, cooking and toilet facilities. Musical instruments were displayed in the shelters and writing materials and games were available. The real learning environment was outside in the garden. This was not an ornamental, suburban or park garden as we think of today, but a children's garden. Visitors of the time were struck by the contrast the garden made with the squalid streets around. McMillan spent much time making this a beautiful oasis; it was designed with the learning of young children at the heart of it. And its relevance to our work today is that it was a planned space where adults played with and helped children. This children's garden was not 'thrown together'; it was not by chance that it was appropriate for young children, it was carefully planned and organised, tended and managed with the learning of children at its heart.

The garden was divided into sections so that there were opportunities to discover, to play, to construct, to garden. Children were able to follow their interests without being interrupted. Staff did not spend anything like as much time as today in setting up activities because children were expected to select them for themselves. The garden was arranged on different levels, on grass and hard surfaces. There were paths, steps, logs, trees, shrubs, ponds, seats, tables, slides, ropes, swings, playhouses, planks, ladders, barrels, blocks. There was a kitchen garden, a wild garden and a rock garden. There was a plethora of natural materials – twigs, leaves, stones, bark, seeds, and so on. The movable equipment included trucks, wheelbarrows and bicycles. Children used real tools. Sand, water and builders' bricks were available. Children had access to dressing-up materials. The garden naturally attracted birds and they were further encouraged with bird boxes, bird baths and bird tables. Animals, including chickens, tortoises, rabbits and fish were kept. Children had access to scientific equipment and to small games apparatus. 'The garden is the essential matter. Not the lessons, or the pictures or the talk. The lessons and talk are about things seen and done in the garden, just as the best of all the paintings in the picture galleries are shadows of the originals now available to children of the open air' (McMillan 1930, p. 2). All activities including movement, singing, painting, meal times and rest took place outside. The fresh air, the physical activity and the space ensured that the children did indeed become healthier (as she had hoped).

Alongside McMillan's writings, the works of Owen (1928), Cusden (1938), de Lissa (1939), Wheeler and Earl (1939) and particularly Isaacs (1932) all add to the general understanding of nursery education in the first half of the nineteenth century. In the garden, experiences were integrated and all aspects of development could be fostered. It was a natural, real-life environment and not a task-structured environment divorced from reality. The pioneers stressed aspects of educational practice which included the importance of space, uninterrupted play, the social aspects of school, the enhancement of corporate activity, and self-initiated play (Owen 1928, Cusden 1938, de Lissa 1939). Learning through play in a natural and interesting environment was seen as the way to help young children develop (Isaacs 1954, McMillan 1930). It was somewhere children naturally wanted to go and was seen to offer first-hand sensory experiences. So, for example, the range of colours could more easily and clearly be studied in the garden rather than by looking at colours on a card. Outdoors is ever-changing and its diversity raises questions. It was also seen as an environment which could encourage 'corporate activity and corporate enjoyment' (Owen 1928, p. 86). Hence the reason the pioneers saw the need for children to play together, and encouraged this by providing scrap materials and movable toys for the children to work with and construct together. De Lissa (1939) talks about children engaging in 'experimental play' (p. 49) with resources such as building materials which have many possibilities, enabling children to put ideas into practice and so practise skills of planning, persistence, concentration and re-evaluation. This was very different from elementary education where all children were expected to do the same thing at the same time. Outdoors offered emotional support, either because it was somewhere feelings could be expressed or because it engendered a feeling of tranquillity. In this environment children were able to benefit from the fresh air. They were able to develop a healthy body alongside a healthy mind, moving about vigorously and being energetic (Plaisted 1909, Holmes and Davies 1937, de Lissa 1939).

Teachers were seen as crucial. 'The whole value of the nursery school will depend, of course, on the teachers. They are the heart of the problem, they can give or withhold success' (McMillan 1919, p. 81). Essentially, it was how the teacher used the theory that made it successful or not, whether interacting with children, setting up an environment for play or involving children in deciding rules and expectations. But McMillan also came to see parents as important and central to the change in people's lives, feeling that the open-air nursery school would draw parents in and they could learn from watching the children at play. She set up the equivalent of a parents' room so they could be educated, being aware that not only the conditions in the slums, but also simple ignorance, created many of the health problems.

Decline of the outdoor play area

Over time, the centrality of the garden to nursery education declined and, with it, the amount of outdoor play also decreased. As early as 1939 concern was being expressed about the misuse of the garden (de Lissa 1939). There seems to be three main reasons why the garden, which was viewed as the *raison d'être* of nursery education, was lost over time. Firstly, nursery education came to be seen as a form of compensatory education, secondly, the provision of nursery education in classes attached to primary schools and not in separate nursery schools and thirdly, the general lack of nursery trained specialists. The impact of these factors was compounded by nursery education never becoming a compulsory phase of education, and the consistent lack of funding which has dogged nursery education since its inception. By 1918, nursery education was on the statute book and this was a major achievement. However, lack of public funding prevented it from becoming universally available. Nursery education has grown over the years, but without overall planning. In some areas there is a good deal of nursery education and in others none at all.

Compensatory education

McMillan and others in the nursery field were very successful in improving the health of young children. They realised that children's health had to be improved before they could be successfully educated; cognitive growth could not be achieved without physical well-being. The emphasis was on outdoor living, with plenty of good food, exercise and rest. In the nursery schools children became healthier and more disease-resistant. As Bradburn (1976) argues in her biography of McMillan, many of McMillan's followers 'may have mistaken the route for the destination' (p. 163). In a sense, the nursery movement's success was also its downfall. As nursery education was seen to dramatically improve the health of children, the conclusion drawn by some was that nursery education was not a new type of education but simply a compensatory education. Put poor, disease-ridden children in the nursery and they will get healthier. Unfortunately, in Government documents, nursery schools came under 'special schools' and this meant they came to be seen as places to help children with special needs, as curative institutions to help some children, but not needed to help all children (Board of Education 1936). Whitbread (1972) argues that the nursery school was seen 'in terms of social and medical care, not as an educational institution' (p. 68). So the garden was not seen as the learning environment but as a health-promoting environment and this is the label still often attached to it.

This compensatory theme continued, and in the 1960s and 1970s nursery education was seen as a solution to educational disadvantage, helping those children who were socially or linguistically disadvantaged. The rise in the 'programme' was evident; it was a case of giving nursery education to the disadvantaged and then they would be better, hence the increase in language programmes. Clark (1988) argues that language was a main justification for the expansion of nursery education at this time. It was seen as a place to prepare children for compulsory schooling, for special needs identification and to some extent it still is. (See Hutt *et al.* (1989) for a discussion of the compensatory tag attached to nursery education.) The significance with regard to outdoor play was that this compensatory education occurred inside the classroom and so the importance of the garden was sidestepped.

Rise of nursery classes

Nursery education started life in schools, separate to the elementary school system. However, over the years, much of the increase in nursery places was in nursery classes attached to primary schools and not in nursery schools. With a drop in the birth rate, primary classrooms would become empty, and so, particularly in the 1930s and again in the 1970s and 1980s, primary classes were often adapted to house a nursery class, this being the cheaper option. On the face of it, this may not be an important change. However, in terms of the centrality of the garden it was highly significant. Immediately, nursery education was about adapting an indoor classroom, not about finding and building a suitable outdoor space. By paying attention to finding a room suitable for the nursery, the outdoor play area was 'relegated from first place in the order of priorities' (McNee 1984, p. 20). Time was taken in finding a room suitable for adaptation, with the minimum amount of cost. Most time, energy and thought would go into the adaptation of the indoor space. The garden was an afterthought, a space to be tacked on. The two areas were not considered together when trying to find the right space for the nursery class. Hence the reason why there are many nursery classes with what can only be described as unusual outdoor areas that are very small, a strange shape, on a slope, with only a hard surface, without shade, without sun, in part of the dustbin area, not even next to the classroom, and so on. The range of nursery outdoor play areas we see today is not a result of considered design, but chance. Because the nursery was part of the elementary or primary school it was affected by it both inside the classroom and very obviously in the use of the outdoor play area.

Teachers who found themselves with such 'interesting' or unusual outdoor play areas had to be very committed to outdoor play to make such areas work. Without this commitment such difficult environments did not get used in the way originally envisaged. Alongside this relegation came terminology relegation and as early as 1936 the garden was being described as the 'playground', where children had 'access to the open air' (Board of Education 1936, p. 20). It is therefore surprising that the outdoor play space still exists at all today. Maybe this points to its centrality and importance to young children's learning.

Lack of trained nursery specialists

Nursery education was seen as different from elementary education and McMillan saw the teacher as the linchpin in the success of children's education. She set up a teacher education college, called the Rachel McMillan Training College, in Deptford, to ensure that nursery teachers had the specialist training required. This was not a version of elementary education but a completely separate training. With the death of nursery pioneers and the lack of universal nursery education the nursery specialist became a rarity.

During both the First and Second World Wars nursery education was increased to free women to do war work. With the ending of both wars there was a dramatic rise in the birth rate and a shortage of primary teachers. After the Second World War, the Government solved this teacher shortage by taking nursery teachers from the nurseries and putting them into the infant classes and replacing them with women who had received a short training in childcare (Blackstone 1971). The training emphasised the care aspect of the work and the fundamental aspects of nursery education, such as the garden, were not taught. During the 1960s there was a general shortage of teachers and the solution was to utilise nursery nurses instead of teachers in the running of the nurseries. On the whole, a nursery nurse training involves the care component of the work far more than the educational aspects. So, again, this has meant that those knowledgeable about nursery education have been few and far between, a situation which has been picked up by many Government documents, including the Education, Science and Arts Committee Report (Great Britain 1988).

The lack of nursery specialists, training students and the consequent lack of specialists in the field, continues to beset nursery and now Foundation Stage education. Today, with an emphasis on subject teaching and increased time in schools, students can still leave college with only a general understanding of the Foundation

Stage and a hazy notion as to what outdoor play is about. Many staff may feel unsure as to the exact nature of nursery education and so provide a primary curriculum instead, with a clear division between work and play, and with the outdoors being relegated to a perceived lower order activity which staff do not get involved in.

In many infant settings, due to a lack of finances, teaching assistants instead of nursery nurses are being employed to work in the Foundation Stage. Newly appointed teaching assistants are receiving a four day training, but this simply covers basic literacy, numeracy and behaviour management; this in no way gives in depth knowledge about young children or how to assist in their learning, as does a two year NNEB qualification. These staff in particular need under-fives training.

Nursery education has always been beset by a lack of funds. The fact that nursery education is not a statutory phase of education means that many people not confident about its true nature may feel very vulnerable and replace nursery education with something closer to primary education. In this climate something as specialised as outdoor play can easily be pushed to the sidelines. However, with the Foundation Stage it is much clearer to all as to what should be provided and how and hopefully outdoor play will be given the status it needs to support children's learning.

Learning from the past

From this brief look at the development of nursery education it can be seen that nursery education did not begin as a sideshoot of primary education and that the garden space is not akin to the primary playground. It is apparent that the outdoor play area is one of those 'traditions' which is unique to nursery education. The garden was central to nursery education and was the main learning area. From looking at the roots of nursery education it is apparent that this space was initially carefully designed and laid out and its use was carefully planned on a daily basis. It was not a place to run about in, after the work had been done inside, it was an area in which children were able to play for the entire session, weather permitting. It was an area where education and care went hand in hand, a wholly new concept at the beginning of the century. It was an area where a healthy body and mind could be developed. It was an environment in which teachers were expected to work and play with children.

The study of the development of nursery education has shown that the centrality of the outdoor learning environment did not decline because it was found to be a useless space, but because external influences brought changes to bear on it. Its centrality declined because nursery education came to be seen as a way to help children who were at a so-called disadvantage, to help with the next phase of education, or to help a child with particular mental or physical needs. In this way, outdoors became an area for physical education and to provide fresh air; indoors for compensating for that so-called disadvantage. It declined in importance because concentrating on providing nursery classes meant that attention was paid to providing indoor spaces and not developing an outdoor learning environment. Therefore, the range of outdoor play areas we see today is not a result of design but chance. One can see the direct influence of infant education, where attention is given entirely to the indoor learning area. Finally, the lack of people knowledgeable about nursery education meant that what went on in many establishments was more akin to infant education, with a division between work and play, with indoors being seen as the work station and outdoors as the much less important play area. In some quarters these attitudes still prevail.

Today

The Start Right report (Ball 1994) recommended the ideal approach to the expansion of nursery education would be based on nursery schools and classes. With the introduction of the desirable learning outcomes and voucher scheme in 1996, the Government was attempting to provide nursery education on the cheap by saying any institution providing care for under-fives, whether it be a playgroup, private/workplace nursery or LEA run nursery could come under the blanket term 'nursery'. Outdoor provision was allowed to decline even further, seen in terms of physical development only and possible to provide in a local authority park.

With the introduction of the Foundation Stage in September 2000, outdoor play has been given prominence and inspections have started to highlight deficiencies in provision and practice. There continues to be a lack of trained nursery/Foundation Stage specialists and this has been particularly apparent since reception children have come under the Foundation Stage umbrella and not the National Curriculum guidance. Teachers are having to make major changes in their thinking as the ways of educating children are unfortunately very different; with an emphasis on play and independence within the Foundation Stage guidance and an emphasis on prescriptive schooling under the National Curriculum. However, many teachers are very keen to make changes and to fully understand the processes behind the Foundation Stage.

Many establishments are making major changes to the actual outdoor play space in the light of the requirements of the Foundation Stage guidance. Some schools have created new outdoor areas and have indeed looked at not only the most appropriate room, but also the best outdoor space for the under-fives. Some LEAs have provided money for fencing. Some schools have been able to fund raise for the outdoor space. Some have been given a limited budget but still been able to make a difference. Hertfordshire LEA has set up an outdoor provision project, which twelve schools are involved in. Importantly there is renewed interest in children learning in an outdoor environment.

Outdoor provision has to been seen as a long-term project, which cannot be rushed. The challenge now is to make sure staff set up an environment that fosters knowledge-seeking behaviour.

4: Design and layout

There is no such thing as a perfectly designed classroom and likewise there is no such thing as a perfectly designed outdoor area. Areas can be too small, too big, too thin, too sprawled out; they can consist of only grass or only tarmac, receive no sun or get no shade, have no shed, and so on. All of these factors will affect the learning and teaching which can go on in the outdoor area. And there are some classes which do not have an outdoor space at all. Whatever the drawbacks of the garden, the best has to be made of the learning environment that is available; compensating for the constraints, exploiting the opportunities.

Some of the difficulties encountered in the outdoor area are created at the design and build stage; such problems can easily be avoided if the outdoor area is considered more carefully when the Foundation Stage class is in its initial design stages. Common difficulties include physical access to the class, the shape of the garden area, shelter from the weather and lack of storage space. Fortunately some of the difficulties can be overcome. So, for example, where access through the outdoor area is causing problems, the access point can be changed. However, changes such as these can be costly. But many difficulties can be diminished by making changes to present practice, or to aspects of organisation and management. Difficulties with access, for example, can be lessened by covering equipment so children do not disturb resources. In this way the design feature is not altered but adapted or worked around to make the outdoor play area more successful. So, where a design feature may seem insurmountable, with a little careful rearrangement of the structure of the day or careful use of staff, this problem can be overcome (see Bilton 1993). In this way difficulties can be erased or diminished; some may of course require more ingenuity than others. As Dowling (1992) argues: 'Nursery design affects how adults and children work' (p. 139); this being the case, staff have to control that environment.

When considering the design features it is of paramount importance to keep the mind focused on the needs of young children. Fisher (1996) argues that effort has to be put into considering what children need and not on the constraints of the environment. She argues that the most important question to ask is: 'What do young learners need most?' (p. 65). This is the starting point for all decisions then made with regard to resources and space. So, when considering the arrangement of the outdoor area it is necessary to ask, given that children have a variety of needs, and class groups vary from year to year:

- what do young children in general need?
- what does this class group need? and
- what do individuals within this class need?

Whatever the outdoor area is like, there are a number of issues which need to be considered at the design stage or when making changes to present practice. These include:

- access to and from the outdoor area,
- size,
- layout,

- fixed equipment,
- the weather,
- surfaces,
- seating,
- the look of the area, and
- storage.

Paying due regard to these issues and making necessary changes will ensure outdoor play is more successful.

Access

Parents, children and staff need to be able to get into the room and also into the garden. Access to the class can either be via an outer door sited in the outdoor play area, via an internal door sited within the school or via an outer door sited outside the nursery garden. In the latter two cases, the outdoor play area can only be accessed via the classroom. In the former case, the class can be accessed via the outdoor play area. It is preferable to have access to the class via a door which is not situated within the outdoor area. If access to the class is through the outdoor area, problems can arise. For example, resources and equipment which have been set up before the start of the session can be moved, changed or disturbed by children and their siblings coming to school. This is not wanton damage, simply changes made by children who see interesting play equipment and want to play. However, if staff have spent time setting up equipment and resources in a particular way for the benefit of the children in their care, not only can the original set-up be lost, but also the possible intended learning outcomes. It can be very disheartening to staff who have spent time setting up to see their work and effort disorganised. If this happens regularly, staff may resort to setting up outdoor play immediately before children are due to go out or, even worse, simply not bothering at all.

The ideal situation has to be access to the establishment through a building, i.e. the classroom and not the garden, with the waiting area for carers and children also being away from the teaching area, whether the indoor classroom or the outdoor area. In this way, children and carers can enter the class, be greeted and then start playing, finally moving to play outside. In this way, equipment carefully and thoughtfully set up by staff cannot be tampered with and the children can begin working with the activities, as the staff had planned.

If it is not possible to deny initial access to the class through the garden and children are likely to disturb equipment already set up, then discussions both with parents and children may help lessen the problem. This is where close contact with parents is so important. But it is difficult for children to see play equipment and stand by and just look at it! Other solutions can be to erect a makeshift fence which almost like an alleyway provides a route which enables children and parents to get into the class but not play with equipment. Schools which have access to the class through the garden have solved the problem by setting up equipment and then covering it over. This is a case of out of sight, out of mind, but it also says that the activities are not to be disturbed. Some classes put small equipment to be used in conjunction with say, the sand, into a box until all the carers have left. It may be that equipment has to be partly set up, but then finally arranged once the carers have left.

Obviously none of these solutions is ideal. It is much better to have the outdoor teaching area only accessible through the classroom, but when it is not, solutions have to be found, so that equipment is not disturbed and the staff's valuable time is not wasted and opportunities lost for children.

Size

Rooms and gardens can be too big or too small, and both can create specific difficulties. In the outdoor area which is too small, children can simply be knocking into each other, ball activities are almost impossible to organise, running and spatial awareness hard to cater for. Lack of space can also affect behaviour. Bates (1996) made a study of children in a playgroup, systematically observing them over a three-month period and found that children's behaviour did change as the number of children increased and so the space available decreased. More crowding led to more aggressive behaviour. Corin Hutt (1972) came to the same conclusions more than 30 years ago when studying three- to eight-year-olds, playing in different group sizes. The larger the group the more aggressive the behaviour towards people and equipment. We therefore need not only to make sure the space is available but that the area is of a generous size. On the other hand, in too large a garden children can feel lost and staff can spend most of the time checking up where everyone is, as opposed to playing with the children. It would be ideal if all outdoor areas were of an optimum size so that children were able to move around freely, without fear of crashing into things or people, and big enough to hold the variety of activities that should be available in the garden but not too spread out. With the introduction of the Foundation Stage new outdoor areas are being built and very sensibly some schools are taking time to really plan out what they want. Where schools are being dictated to by architects and builders, staff are once again having problems created for practice.

A small space

An outdoor play area can be very small, but when viewed in conjunction with the indoor area, can become a reasonable sized space. In the Bilton (1993) study, it was found that the difficulties created by a garden being too small for 26 children to work in at once, were immediately overcome by accepting one of the principles of outdoor play, as highlighted in the Introduction: namely, that indoors and outdoors are a combined environment and that both are available at the same time. So a small outdoor space can be made much more useful and manageable if available in conjunction with indoors. It is highly unlikely that all children will want to go outdoors at once, but will pass from activity to activity, moving from indoors to outdoors as need arises. In nurseries which have small outdoor areas, but where staff consider outdoors and indoors together, it is indeed rare for an area to become full with children. If the garden does reach saturation point then children will have to be asked to come back later. They are very accepting when told a maximum of 'four children at the water tray', so they can accept 'only x number of children in the garden'. It is obviously not an ideal situation but still effective. It may be that there is limited space both outside and inside, and by using the two areas simultaneously cramped space conditions inside are improved upon.

What about the garden which is so small that it is impossible to have a balance of activities going on at the same time? This can also happen inside, with the very small classroom. In this situation, it is a case of considering what activities the children should be experiencing and then providing them. Starting from the premise that one cannot provide all activities as the space is too small, will mean that the space constraints dictate the curriculum; starting with the needs of the children and then working out how best to provide for them will ensure that the teacher, and not the space, is in charge of the curriculum. If you are trying to offer a balanced curriculum then you need to offer it despite the restrictions. Many nursery schools do not have a school hall; this does not mean, however, that music and movement is abandoned; instead, ways of providing for it have to be found. It is a case of allocating different time or space to accommodate the relevant activities; furniture and equipment, may well have to be moved out of the way for the session and replaced when the movement lesson has finished.

Young children are physically active, and where a classroom and outdoor area are small, children still have a right to be physically active. In order to maximise space, it may be necessary to remove superfluous furniture from indoors and oudoors. If small apparatus skills are considered a relevant and meaningful component of the curriculum, but the space available is too small, then ways around the situation need to be considered; for example, the primary playground could be utilised when the older children are not using it. All the children may have to go into the area and practise small apparatus skills. This is not the best approach, but it may be the only option available. However, it is important to ensure this experience is regular, otherwise all that has been learned in one session will be lost by the time the next session comes about.

If imaginative play is seen as essential, then it may be possible to use the outdoor area exclusively for this and other activities such as vigorous activity may have to be timetabled inside daily, similar to a timetabled PE lesson. Or again, it could be that the primary playground is used for the vigorous activity with one member of staff inside, one member of staff with the children in the outdoor area and one in the primary playground. Bikes can create problems in a small outdoor play area and it may be best simply to dispense with them. The skills involved in bike riding can be catered for to a degree, through climbing and running games, and it may be better to encourage group rather than solitary play by having a truck in the garden which children can use together. If seen as an essential experience, bikes could be provided at a separate time or again in the primary playground. Gardening work may have to be organised on a rota basis, with one group of children at a time doing the work. Tubs, plant pots and boxes can all be used for seeds, bulbs and plants if there is no garden space.

A large space

When a garden space is large it is important to consider carefully how children and staff will respond to it, bearing in mind studies such as Sylva *et al.* (1980) and Smith and Connelly (1981) which concluded that children found it harder to settle and play in large open spaces and in larger groups. Neill (1982) found that, in large open space, adults tended to oversee a range of activities rather than become involved with specific children. This view was highlighted by a teacher in the Bennett *et al.* (1997) studies who felt too much space was difficult to manage without additional help.

The larger nursery garden is often associated with the nursery school setting which may have a number of classes accessing one garden as opposed to the nursery class, attached to the primary school, which will only have one class accessing one outdoor play area. In the case of a nursery school with a number of classes accessing one outdoor area, thought does need to be given to the best use of this space. It may be worth considering dividing the area so that each class does, in fact, have a designated piece of garden, an extension of their classroom, with the rest of the space as free access to all children. This can often be seen in nurseries built prior to, or during, the Second World War with the outdoor space immediately outside the classroom possessing not only a veranda but also dividing walls between the classes.

One concern with a large and totally open space is that it can become similar to an infant/junior playground. Children can feel lost in such a large space, play can become somewhat frantic and less developed and it is very difficult from the staff's point of view not only to evaluate children at work, but also to play with and teach them. It is rare to find actual classrooms for 60 or 80 plus children, because it is felt children need smaller numbers in order to feel secure. Even in an open-plan situation, where children might be working in fairly large groups, children usually have a home base, a smaller known area, which is theirs.

Outside needs to be viewed in the same light and in some spaces it may be worth considering breaking up a large outdoor area, which is accessed by a large number of children and creating home bays outside. It may be appropriate to divide the whole garden so that each class has its own garden area with a repeat of all or some of the activities and equipment within each area, although of course this may be restricted by cost. Where a school does have a large outdoor space accessible by children from all classes, staff need to be very attentive in their observations of the children and be able to talk easily as a staff group.

The size of the outdoor area can affect the work of children and adults; it is therefore necessary for staff to look at this issue to see if the size of the area is supporting or adversely affecting the quality of the play. Each group of children is unique and has particular needs and it may be necessary to make changes to design features. If social interaction is important, it may be more effective to create separate gardens to enable children to work and play in small groups. If the group is needing lots of vigorous activity then it may be necessary to create home bays just outside the classroom which have some activities that are the same, for example, imaginative play materials, building and game resources. These home bays then open out into the communal garden area, for all the children to use climbing, running and balancing equipment. It may be that the areas can be divided by time, for example children could have access to their class and outdoor area for the first hour of free play and then the rest of the garden area could be opened to everyone. It may be that children are not playing effectively or cooperatively in the communal area and dividing the outdoors so that each class has a specific area, may result in the arguments and conflicts simply melting away.

Layout

Within a classroom there will be different areas for different activities. Foundation Stage and infant classrooms are divided to accommodate different activities: curriculum areas across the space are catered for. A classroom is not left as an empty open room, similar to a hall. Therefore, for the outdoor area to be a learning and teaching environment it cannot be left as an empty space. It has to be treated in the same way as a classroom and what is provided in the outdoor area and where activities are positioned all need careful consideration. It is also necessary to consider how areas can be divided, what activity works best next to what activity, where the main walkways are, and whether the area is inviting to children.

A study by Brown and Burger (1984) found that design issues which were important in affecting play in the outdoor area were:

- 'zoning' (positioning of equipment),
- 'encapsulation' (enclosing areas for separate activities), and
- the provision of appropriate equipment (e.g. vehicles).

In one playground, there was no play at the sand box because it was positioned in a high traffic area. Anyone who has visited an outdoor play area where children on bikes are rushing around will know how frightening this feels and how it can completely hinder play by other children. In the playground which promoted the highest levels of desirable social, motor and language behaviours and the highest rates of equipment involvement, there were many enclosed areas; children had plenty of opportunities to use vehicles, they had space and the correct surfaces to use these vehicles. Also, the play structures there offered greater opportunities for physical activity and offered more variety of use by children. The playground with the lower ratings of children's behaviour *seemed* to have a lot going for it except that:

- there was too much emphasis on it being aesthetically pleasing,
- it had a large play structure, and a playhouse,
- the ground was terraced,
- there was a vehicle path and a large area with painted lines designed for play with vehicles.

The conclusion of the authors was that there was too little the children could actually change in this playground and so the play was at a lower level. The designers had done too much. This is a view echoed by research into the designing of a nursery class garden (Bilton 1994). This particular outdoor area had clear paths to follow, extensive planting and was lovely to look at; the paths and flower beds, however, limited where children could move and almost prohibited the use of wheeled toys as the path was too winding. In many ways the school had done too much to this nursery outdoor play area, the space was very controlled and little was left for the children to affect.

In essence then the outdoor area needs to be a free space in which staff can create the learning bays that they want. So there needs to be an area for:

- imaginative play,
- building and construction,
- physical activity,
- the use of smaller motor skill activities,
- horticultural work,
- scientific and environmental discovery, and
- quiet play.

These are the essential areas, but more can be added depending on the actual shape, size and so on, of the outdoor area and the needs of each group of children. These areas for learning or learning bays are discussed in greater detail in the next chapter.

There will need to be boundaries between the learning bays, mostly created by the clustering of resources or the placing of a resource trolley or arrangement of equipment. Sometimes a more permanent boundary can be created using a hedge or trellis with plants growing up. This may be grown to protect the gardening section, where seeds and plants grown to be harvested cannot be dug up in a game of treasure hunt! Or it may be that a quiet spot is needed and hedging or trellising can help create this tranquil spot. But permanent boundaries tend to be the exception rather than the rule, given the need for children to be able to have an effect on their learning environment by changing it and the need for staff to organise the environment as they wish.

Which activity is placed next to which will depend on such things as mess, space, safety, number of children, noise and so on. Teets (1985) argues that the activity to take place should be considered before determining where to locate that particular centre. Some of these considerations will change from day to day and week to week, while some considerations such as safety, will be permanent – ball games cannot be played on a boundary next to a road or unprotected window(s). However, there are ways round such difficulties; one simple remedy could be to provide soft, light balls for children to use. Positioning a quiet activity near the nursery building, such as a table activity or sand play, can encourage those children who feel rather apprehensive about play in the outdoors to venture out, be seen to be playing but at the same time watching what is going on in the rest of the play area. The movement of children's play will need to be monitored to see where the natural walkways are and to make sure they are not creating difficulties.

Fixed equipment

In recent times, more and more nurseries have purchased large play structures and playhouses similar to those found in playgrounds in public parks. In part, this may have occurred as staff, unsure about outdoor play, have seen such fixtures as filling the void of insecurity. It is often considered a good way of bringing parents together for a very evident funding-raising scheme. This type of permanent fixture is rarely apparent in the class inside. Although they may be of use in the public park it is doubtful whether they are of much use for the learning of young children in the early years setting. The study by Brown and Burger (1984) found that the playground with the most fixed equipment and which looked very pleasing, had in fact the lower rating of play. The difficulty with the fixed play structure was that only a finite number of movements were possible and children had no opportunities to change it. What the children had in the playground with the highest play rating was equipment which they could manoeuvre, which had a number of approaches, and a variety of differing areas. Playgrounds which encouraged good quality play had features such as linkages of equipment, flexible material – those which can be changed, manipulated or combined, graduated challenges and a variety of possible experiences (Johnson, Christie and Yawkey 1987).

Blatchford (1989), looking into playgrounds in the primary school, argues that the 'contemporary' playground equipment can do little to help children develop and may even do less than the 'traditional' equipment. A study by Walsh (1993), looking at outdoor play in Australia, and referring to research both there and in the USA, argues that fixed playground equipment is of little use with young children. She points to research which shows that children prefer creative playgrounds; action-orientated equipment over fixed equipment, because the resources can be adapted to suit the children's play ideas. In this study, the fixed equipment was used for less time and in less complex ways. Frost and Campbell (1985) found primary-aged children preferred movable and complex equipment which had a number of options and could be used in a variety of ways. This was because children could change it rather than have to adapt their play to the limitation of static equipment. The beautifully designed and costly climbing apparatus stretches the designer's imagination, but does little to stretch the child's. Sometimes it is possible to do too much, to build something too perfect, so the child has little to do. Blocks may not look good or real, but the possibilities for their use are endless. Equipment needs to be simple, natural, unlimiting, interpretable, movable and adaptable (Miller 1972).

Barbour (1999) made a study of two school playgrounds in Texas for use by children during their break time. One playground was what is described as traditional and had such things as seesaws, jungle gyms, slide, all of which were simply for exercise. The other playground had much more variety of equipment and included a play structure with lots of parts – tunnels, bridge, rings, wide platform, steering wheel, overhead ladder, plus various loose parts-building blocks, wooden planks, plastic spools, tools, chairs, containers and sandpit, playhouses, garden area. The equipment in this playground was often designed for more than one child. The author looked at the children with both high and low physical competence and concluded that the playground that emphasised physical play tended to segregate children and stopped some children being able to socialise. Competitive play rather than cooperative play was being encouraged in the traditional playground with fixed equipment. She argues that playgrounds that support a range of play types help 'foster the social involvement of all children regardless of (their) level of motor proficiency' (p. 95). So this study found that the equipment provided actually affected social development and as a consequence must have been affecting personal and emotional development. It seems fairly obvious really, but if we want all children to attempt to work together we need to provide them with equipment that helps that, not just equipment that some children can use confidently. She further argues that playgrounds that focus on physical skill are giving high status to those who can achieve this and low status to those who cannot. Although this study is dealing with primary playgrounds, the findings are relevant to the Foundation Stage as it deals with fixed equipment versus movable.

If a fixed play structure has been inherited then consideration will need to be given as to how it can be added to, so it becomes more complex. For fixed equipment to be of use to young children it needs to have loose parts which children can attach themselves and thereby change the structure (Walsh 1993). The old-fashioned smaller non-permanent fixed climbing frame has this potential. Complexity has to be the key to sustaining a child's interest, enjoyment and development and needs to be built into play provision (Frost 1986). Enabling children to incorporate planks, ladders and resources so that they can make spaceships, boats, homes, building sites, and so on, may be one way round the problem. Sometimes this is not possible as the bars on the fixed play structure are too wide and homemade planks and ladders will have to be made. Likewise, playhouses can look good, but can often be quite small inside and can be very expensive. These fixed houses can be poorly used as there is little equipment provided. Just as with any role-play area children need to be inspired by a focus and need good resources to play with. So, for example, the house could be a fairy tale castle, a home, a florist, a railway station waiting room, with all the necessary paraphernalia associated with that particular setting. A florist could have flowers, large vases, paper, sticky tape, till, money, ribbon and scissors. This play could then flow into the rest of outdoors and indoors. Bikes could have baskets or boxes attached to the front bars to hold flowers for delivery. If staff show interest in an area, by resourcing it and working in it, children will do also. If a house has one table, one chair and a broken bed it says to children 'we don't care, so why should you'. It may be possible to change the playhouse so it is a quiet area for drawing, writing and collage work.

A fixed structure can mean that staff feel obliged to include it in the planning, and then list what activities it might be used for. Unfortunately, in such a situation it is the equipment which is controlling the curriculum. It would be more effective to list the learning bays or areas of learning and then see how such permanent structures can be incorporated into the various bays or areas. However, it may be necessary to actually get rid of such items, if they are taking up too much valuable space.

Blatchford (1989) issues a word of warning about purchasing fixed equipment. He suggests that the purchase of costly outdoor equipment is often not based on clear research, as the purchase of indoor equipment generally is. Instead it is more likely to be a hit and miss affair, with a hope that the children will like it. For the class or school it can be not only costly but also take up a major part of the outdoor area. Young children need space and this can be greatly affected by the fixing of a huge play structure. The only well-used piece of fixed equipment is monkey bars. Recently, this conclusion was borne out by a school that has both climbing frame and monkey bars; they found the latter was still used after many years but not the former. Another school found children initially keen to use a newly installed climbing frame but two years later no interest was shown in this hugely costly item. In conclusion, it would seem that the buying of a fixed piece of equipment, for example, a play structure, a swing, or a playhouse, needs to be considered very carefully and will most likely be low on the list of priorities as its use in an educational setting is limited. The amount such items cost has to be balanced against how much quality play comes from them. The more versatile a piece of equipment or resource, the more uses it has and therefore the more cost effective it is. A-frames, planks, material and boxes will afford much more continual play than a fixed structure.

Slopes

A very versatile shape in a Foundation Stage outdoor area is a slope. A steep grassed slope can be used to manoeuvre oneself or objects up and down. Its shape lends itself to encouraging cooperative play, for example when pushing a truck up the hill. It is safe and can offer major challenge with little chance of danger. It can give as much a thrill to be at the top of a steep slope as being at the top of a climbing frame. A rope can be securely fixed into the ground at the top, to aid with the moving up and down. If there is potential to have a slope then it would be beneficial to fund raise for one.

The weather

The most unpredictable component of working outside is undoubtedly the weather! However, it has to be worked with so that children do not miss out. In terms of design and layout it is important to take into consideration all possible permutations of

Figure 4.1 Versatile resources and equipment. This rope was strung between two trees for swinging and moving along using hands and feet.

weather, including rain, sun, wind, extreme heat and extreme cold. Obviously with the latter two types of weather, protection can be offered in the form of clothing and creams. But, given the damaging effects of the sun's rays on young children, it is important to offer further protection through structures which offer shade and shelter. It is surprising still to see primary-aged children playing out at lunchtime in blistering heat without any shade.

When building a new class or redesigning an old one it is necessary to consider which part of the school grounds is most protected from the wind, sun and cold. Some outdoor areas are unusable even by the toughest of children and staff because of the wind. Strong and persistent wind can impinge on play and concentration and such an environment is not conducive to learning. The outdoor area needs to be protected from the wind either by buildings, fencing, trees and shrubs or a combination of these. Although a south facing area is lovely it needs a great deal of protection with good shade, otherwise it will be too hot. Nurseries in Frankfurt are always built so the garden is south facing, but then shade is created (Bergard 1995). At the other extreme, a garden in total shade can be a harsh environment to work in. Ideally then, an outdoor area which receives some sun and some shade is the best. When considering the needs of part-time children, both sessions need to benefit from the sun and shade. Faced with an established outdoor area which is affected by climatic difficulties, it is necessary to ascertain how the outdoor area can be protected firstly from the wind and sun. Protection from the rain, so children can go out if it is raining, has to come at a later stage.

In an ideal world there would be a veranda or covered way, so that children can play outside whatever the weather. Many older nurseries have one, but not many schools or classes built today have. The nursery pioneers considered the veranda an essential component of the nursery, so that children could be out in the fresh air whatever the weather. Many nurseries built years ago also had sliding doors so that one side of the nursery could open out completely. In Australia it is the norm to have a veranda: 'In common with many Australian preschool buildings, there was no firm distinction between indoors and out. Sliding doors created an easy flow from playroom to patio to playground' (McLean 1991, p. 71). If money is available or if the parent group wishes to have a specific item to raise funds for, a veranda or covered way would be ideal. A cheaper option could be a shop awning which can be pulled out when needed.

Pergolas are another way of offering protection in the outdoor area. These can either be attached to the class outside or built as a separate fixture in the garden. The siting needs careful consideration as it should not take over the garden. Climbing plants trained up the sides can soon give an enclosed feel to the pergola and if trained across the top can offer some protection from the elements. A thick canvas or bamboo sheeting across the top can be used to offer greater protection from the rain, wind and sun. Children can incorporate such a structure into their play, and use blocks and crates to make a hidey-hole.

Trees are not as useful for offering protection from the rain but do offer good shade from the sun. Whether taking over a class or setting up a new one it is important to

Figure 4.2 Reading outside, whatever the weather.

have trees planted as soon as possible. The longer the delay, the longer it will take to get the shelter benefits. A reasonable sized tree purchased from a garden centre should be offering protection within three years.

It is always possible to rig up makeshift protection outside, whether there is already permanent protection in the area or not. For example, a sheet of canvas can be strung up attached to a fence, tree, shrub or wall close at hand. Climbing frames, A-frames or even ladders attached horizontally can be draped with material to offer shade. Another possibility is a large umbrella, like those found on beaches. These can offer shade from the sun and in winter some degree of shelter and can act as rest spots for children for imaginative play purposes, games or simple quiet reflection.

Surfaces

It is preferable to have different surfaces in the outdoor area, just as there are different surfaces within the class, including carpet, lino and tiles. With different surfaces different activities can be offered. A hard surface is probably the best type of flooring for the area in front of the class or access point, so that children can always go out and use the area even if the grass is like a quagmire.

A hard surface is better for manoeuvring wheeled vehicles on. Naylor (1985) looked at various studies which reveal that children prefer hard surfaces because they can use wheeled toys easily on such a surface. It can be easier to build on a hard surface, but it can be a problem with varnished wooden surfaces, such as found on the blocks, as they can get scratched and splintered. The grass is a better surface for the gymnasium and for actually sitting on, as it is softer! Imaginative play works well on either surface. If there is only a hard surface and no earth, then plants and shrubs can be planted in pots, tubs or any container which will hold soil. Where there is no grass, it is necessary to provide carpet squares or pieces of thick material for children to sit on and to use as gathering spots. Long term, it is preferable to get a hard surface if there is none and similarly a grassed or a soil area if none exists already.

Some settings have had a shock absorbent surface built which can then be used for any piece of equipment, not just for one fixed climbing frame. In this way the safety surface is more flexible and the staff can use it as they wish. The school described in case study 3 (Chapter 2) built a 10m x 13m rectangular safety surface toward the middle of the outdoor area, for the use of A-frames, planks and other moveable climbing equipment.

A common cry is that of wet grass and shoes either making a mess or causing children to slip. In one class, children were not allowed to go on the grass when it was wet; however, the grass took up most of the garden space and if children went out it was difficult for them not to use this space. In this sort of situation it is worth thinking about getting rid of some of the grass and creating a hard surface, otherwise children and staff spend valuable time in 'get off the grass' conversations. Wellingtons can be a solution in that children can change into them quickly if it is wet and/or muddy outside. Children can soon learn to wash down boots in a bowl of water with a long-handled scrubbing brush. Children will only find out about muddy areas and how to walk on them if they are allowed to experience them. Viewing each day separately and deciding whether children can go on the grass or need boots, will ensure that the outdoor area is used as much as possible. Blanket rules about 'no one on the grass in winter', mean a valuable resource is lost.

Seating

One of the noticeable differences about some outdoor areas in comparison to others is the distinct lack of seating. It is, therefore, not surprising that some staff find it tiring working in the outdoor play area and some children find it daunting when there is no seating. Having somewhere to sit has a significant and immediate impact on the play within the outdoor area; it also helps staff feel happier about working out there. I've never understood why we don't have seating outside, inside we would not be expected to stand up all day. It is essential to have a variety of seating: chairs from inside can be used outside, or child chairs can be purchased specifically for use outside. Crates with planks balanced across can act as a seat, so too can a large tyre. However, it is important to use seating which is movable, so that it can be used as children and staff wish it to be used. A proper garden seat can be added, but in some areas it may have to be fixed to the ground so it cannot be stolen.

How the outside area looks

One of the difficulties with the outdoor area is in making it look nice; a difficulty highlighted by the Gilkes (1987) study. It is not easy to make something which consists of tarmac look attractive. At the end of the day when everything has been put away, there is little to show in an outdoor area in comparison to the inside, with displays, equipment and so on, all about the room. Outdoors can look miserable on a cold, damp day. When children have been playing industriously outside, to the visitor it can simply look chaotic and a mess! Naturally staff want indoors and outdoors to look aesthetically pleasing.

However, it is important not to equate aesthetically pleasing with stimulating. What is aesthetically pleasing to us may not be of much use to young children. The outdoor play area is not a suburban garden, with its carefully tended rose beds, nor is it a play park with an attractive wooden play structure. It is a working environment for young children and as such it needs to look stimulating, that is, have activities for children to work with. It needs to be exciting, and in order for this to be so, it needs to have resources and equipment which have unlimited possibilities.

Obviously it is important to make the outdoor class look as attractive as possible so that children and staff want to go into the environment and feel tranquil in the setting. This can be achieved with the planting of shrubs and trees, the use of good quality equipment and the careful laying out of the resources and equipment. Gilkes (1987) discusses how, what she describes as 'one of the most sterile and unattractive play areas one could imagine', was transformed (p. 73). She is realistic and discusses how much harder it is to effect change in the outdoor area, but with a good deal of time, effort, money, staff and parental involvement plus help from other adults, the area was changed and made a more interesting and appealing area. The teacher in case study 2 (Chapter 2) 'beautified' her outdoor area, as she felt it was too much of a dead space, a thoroughfare and although it was going to be continued to be used as a walkway between her classes and hall it needed to be made significantly different to show it was now a teaching and learning area. The list of possible plants is endless, but Figure 4.3 gives a few examples of easy growing plants and trees.

Figure 4.3

Alder
Birch
Buddleia
Clematis (*Montana*)
Flowering quince (*Chaenomeles speciosa*)
Forsythia
Hebe
Jew's Mallow (*Kerria*)
Juniper (*Juniperus*)
Lavender (*Lavandula angustifolia*)
Mexican orange blossom (*Choisya ternata*)
Oak
Rosemary (*Rosemarinus officinalis*)
Tree mallow (*Lavatera*)
Weigela
Willow

If three tree plants are put in the same hole and the leaders taken out, this will quite quickly give good coverage.

See Cooper and Johnson (1991) for a list of poisonous plants.

Storage

Outdoor equipment can be big, bulky and cumbersome and consequently needs considerable space for storage. Both the Gilkes (1987) and Bilton (1993) studies highlighted staff concerns about moving outdoor equipment; this is made doubly difficult if there is no shed. In this case it can mean staff are required to move equipment long distances and around awkward spaces. The lack of a shed can be a hindrance to the use of the outdoor play area, as the movement of equipment can be difficult, while the use of indoor areas to store equipment can decrease the amount of usable space inside.

Without a shed it is worth looking at the present equipment and considering what is not used much, what is perhaps not very versatile and so can be dispensed with and replaced by more versatile and less cumbersome equipment, such as imaginative play resources, bricks instead of crates or fewer bikes. In this way the lack of a shed is not so problematic in terms of moving equipment about, as the reduced amount and size of equipment is easier to handle. This can be further helped by viewing outdoor play, not just in terms of physical development, but also in terms of all-round development. If the area is not prone to vandalism, things made of plastic, aluminium and coated metal can be left outside, but would need periodic cleaning and checking.

If it is possible to have a shed this should be organised, so maximising the space available, with shelves and hooks and labels. Staff need to view the shed as any other storage space, which children can access. Trolleys for the various learning bays can be put in position outside and once play has finished can be put back in the central space of the shed. Even a shoulder-height shed can house quite an amount of equipment.

In conclusion

Foundation Stage outdoor areas vary greatly, some are just right, some have difficulties which were created at the building stage and some have difficulties which are created by the misuse of the area. At the design and building stage, planners need to be more concerned with the size of space given over to the outdoor play area, its layout, and the effects of weather. It is not sufficient just to tack on the outdoor play space to the classroom allocated for the early years children. Planners also need to make sure they do not build too many controlling features, such as vehicle paths or fixed play structures. The size of the garden should be sufficient to enable all children to work in comfort and move at speed. A basic rectangular shape, with both grass and hard surfaces available is probably the easiest outdoor area to work with. With this basic shape, staff can then create the learning bays themselves. A place for the storage of equipment, although not essential, reduces the workload of the staff. They can then spend their time creating interesting activities for the children, rather than moving furniture from one place to another. Access to the classroom through the garden is not a good idea as this also creates unnecessary work for the staff.

When looking at an established outdoor area, consideration needs to be given to all the issues raised in this chapter:

- the layout,
- the amount of space available,
- the way the environment is arranged,
- the use of fixed equipment,
- the effects of the weather,
- the need for storage.

All of these issues will affect the quality of play which can be offered. As Barbour (1999) argues, 'playground design influences children's physical competence, play behaviors, and ultimately their peer relationships' (p. 96) and Frost (1992) argues that some outdoor learning environments more effectively support children's growth and development than others. Some changes will take longer to introduce than others, for example, supplying a safety surface or covered way, while others may be solved fairly quickly, for example, providing makeshift shelters or setting up outside so that incoming children do not disturb equipment. There are many features of outdoor areas which designers and planners and staff need to take into consideration, but it is also important that adults do not do too much, so that children end up with a space which may look good but cannot be affected and changed by them. It is the children's imaginations which need stretching, not those of the adults.

Further reading

Dudek, M. (1996) *Kindergarten Architecture.* London: Chapman and Hall.

Although this book is about nursery school buildings around the world, it is a fascinating book and there is pertinent information concerning design and layout for both indoors and outdoors.

5: Learning bays

When a teacher takes over a new class the first thing to do is look at the environment to see how it will work for them. Given a brand new classroom they are unlikely to leave it as an empty space, but are more likely to start to divide the room up into separate units or areas for learning: the book corner, a painting area, an investigative area or blockplay area. Hutt *et al.* (1989) describe these areas for learning as 'micro-environments', meaning environments which are created for a special activity or purpose. This term is further discussed by McAuley and Jackson (1992) and Robson (1996). Nash (1981) uses the term 'learning centres' to describe the areas which have been organised within the spatially planned classroom and Cole (1990) uses the term 'activity center'. Henniger (1993/4) citing Esbensen (1987) uses the term 'zones' when describing outdoor play in US preschools.

My own preference is for the term 'learning bay', which describes an activity area, or an area for learning, each of which having a slightly different focus. What is important here is not so much the words used but that outdoor play has to be seen in terms not of one open space, but a number of areas divided for learning, just as in the indoor area. In this way the whole curriculum can be on offer and the focus of the learning bays helps to ensure that a balance of activities is available and that the teaching potential of all activities has been considered. For outdoor play to be successful this arrangement of learning bays, learning areas, micro-environments, zones, centres, or whatever you wish to call them, is essential. Outdoors we need to be specific about how, and what, we are providing for the children.

Inside, the whole curriculum is offered across the room. This is the approach anticipated in the outdoor class, covering, as a guide, the nine areas of learning and experience:

- linguistic and literacy;
- aesthetic and creative;
- human and social;
- mathematical;
- moral;
- physical;
- scientific;
- technological;
- spiritual.

(Great Britain 1989)

Also covering the six areas of learning:

- personal, social and emotional development;
- communication, language and literacy;
- mathematical development;
- knowledge and understanding of the world;
- physical development;
- creative development.

(QCA 2000)

Learning bays help to ensure all curriculum areas are covered. However, outdoors cannot be a copy of indoors for obvious reasons. Some materials, such as paper, can be difficult to use outside, but it will need to be utilised differently (for example, by using clipboards) thereby ensuring children have access to writing and drawing when outdoors. But it will also not be a copy of indoors because the outdoors lends itself more to some activities than others: it is much easier to make a mess outside, much simpler to throw a ball outdoors, it is less disturbing to make a noise outdoors and easier to manoeuvre large play equipment.

However, that does not mean that outdoors is relegated to an area where only children's physical development is enhanced, but it is an area where a very accessible mode of learning is possible: learning through movement. Returning to the guiding principles in the Introduction, indoors and outdoors need to be used by the children in a combined way, some children find it easier to work outside and so access the curriculum there. So not only do the learning bays provide for specific learning which cannot take place inside, they also provide the same learning opportunities as those which can take place inside.

Esbensen (1987) suggests there needs to be seven play zones outside. These are:

- transition,
- manipulative/creative,
- projective/fantasy,
- focal/social,
- social/dramatic,
- physical, and
- natural element.

By providing these he argues that staff can ensure children have a variety of play types to participate in. Hutt *et al.* (1989) discuss areas for physical, fantasy and material play. The Inner London Education Authority (ILEA) document discusses the need for large and small equipment, imaginative play materials, wheeled toys, environmental materials, blocks and building materials and natural materials (Lasenby 1990). Within this document a planning sheet from a school divides the outdoor area into scientific, imaginative, physical and construction areas. Manning and Sharp (1977) describe four categories of play for both indoors and outdoors. These are domestic, construction, make-believe, natural materials plus one extra for outdoors – play stimulated by the outside environment.

Hill (1978) describes four categories of play and play space outdoors – physical, social, creative and quiet. Gallahue (1989) discusses five areas outside, one for large muscle activities, one for experience with various media, one for seclusion and quiet activities, one for opportunities to observe nature, and one for opportunities to dramatise real-life experiences. I suggest the need for a number of basic learning bays, which can be added to, dependent on the needs of the children, just as indoors. These include:

- an imaginative play area,
- a building and construction area,
- a gymnasium area,
- a small apparatus area,
- a horticultural area,
- an environmental and science area, and
- a quiet area.

These areas cover the three important modes of learning: movement, play and sensory experience. For this organisation to work there needs to be a degree of flexibility in and between bays and between outdoors and indoors, and plentiful resources. There also needs to be some continuity, so activities can be ongoing from day to day.

Flexibility

It is not sufficient to just provide these learning bays: how they are used is important to children's learning. The learning bays have to be seen as flexible and a part of the whole learning environment and not as isolated units. Children need to know that they can move their play from one bay to the next and that they will be able to continue their play scene; they also need to know that materials can be moved from one bay to another. The only provisos are that children should not impede other children in their play, interrupt them, put other children or themselves in danger, or damage equipment. McAuley and Jackson (1992) argue that when organising space, the micro-environments need to be arranged so that activities are combined within them, but not so rigidly that children are unable to combine materials within and between the various learning centres. Children can be thwarted in their play simply because they are not allowed to move something from one area to the next. Hutt *et al.* (1989) describe how some staff would not allow the mixing of micro-environments, so, for example, a cake made of sand could not be allowed in the home corner. The authors suggest that this is a pity as children are being prevented from making connections in their understanding. This type of attitude is apparent in some early years settings where nothing is allowed to be mixed or moved, so that children are not able to develop ideas or use their imaginations. Athey (1990) concludes that children do explore system-atically and have 'schemas of action' and they need to follow their particular interests and concerns. Matthews (1994), discussing visual representation, describes how Ben followed an interest and both drew and built 'fire'. This child mixed drawing materials and toys, such as blocks, straws and a sleeping bag. It was an ongoing project/sculpture and the child's thinking would have been disrupted if it had been cleared away everyday. Matthews argues that children need to be able to mix toys and materials and need time for these often individual projects to develop and so be left out. Fundamental to this has to be enabling children to move play and materials between these learning bays.

Moving from indoors to outdoors

For children's understanding to be successful they need to know they can move their play and materials from indoors to outdoors and vice versa. Children's learning can be equally thwarted if told: 'You can't take that outside, it's an inside dolly' or 'That pushchair cannot go in the house, it's an outside pushchair'. It may not be possible to allow complete freedom of movement of materials between these two environments but there is scope for a good deal of flexibility. Bringing bikes and trucks inside may not be possible in some classes as it may be physically impossible to get them through the door, or the space inside may be just too restrictive. However, in the Hartley (1993) research one school did allow tricycles both indoors and outdoors, even though the space was limited. What is allowed needs to be agreed with the children and made clear to them, so that they know the reason for the rules. The rules have to be there for the benefit of children's learning: 'No dollies outside because they might get dirty' does not seem a sufficiently good reason for them not to be taken outdoors. In the Nash (1981) study the randomly-arranged classrooms used 'housekeeping' criteria to decide how the space was organised, whereas the structured class used 'educational' criteria, which reflected learning objectives.

Although it is important to work within agreed rules, it is also important to be flexible and in some circumstances it may be appropriate to bend, or simply not follow, the rule. For example, for the sake of enabling a particular play scene to continue, a bike might be allowed inside, when this is normally not permissible. In such circumstances talking to children about a decision is important. By being flexible, each situation can be taken on its merits. In this way, each can be looked at in terms of what the learning possibilities are if it is allowed, what they are if it is not, what long-term damage may be caused, and so on. Following the path of flexibility means that children can, for example, have an imaginative house-decorating and moving scene where they can build with blocks outside, decorate the blocks with wallpaper using adhesive tape, add furniture from the inside home corner and bring cakes made from the sand in the sandpit.

Similarly, children can go from being builders outside, moving inside to make and write signs, moving back outside to set up the signs. If children are not allowed to move their play from outdoors to indoors and back again, if they are not allowed to use materials from more than one area this quality of play and learning cannot occur. Even in winter such play can occur, but the children need to be dressed up warmly. It is much more difficult when it is wet and the only outside surface is grass, because of the problem of muddy shoes but children can take their shoes off while the play goes on inside and then put their shoes or wellington boots on when moving back outside. This is not ideal, but a means whereby children are still allowed to follow their play and interests.

Most classes who operate a combined indoor and outdoor area, tend to devote the first ten minutes or so of the session to greeting parents and carers and leave the outdoor area closed. Once the initial rush is over and parents are not needing the close attention of the staff, then the door to the outside area is opened. But this is a quiet affair, and no announcement is made. One member of staff may ask two or three children to come out, or it may be that children naturally gravitate to the door as the parents disperse. This opening has to be a quiet affair so the children who are involved inside are not disturbed. Sometimes it can happen that children are so engrossed inside that they do not venture out until much later in the session and on some days many children will want to start outside straight away. Each day will be different. If there are a lot of staff it may be appropriate to have outdoors open from the beginning of the session.

Resources

Just as with the indoor space, each bay outside needs to have the relevant resources at hand, in trays, boxes or shelving, so that they are accessible and easily used by the children. It may be that the class does not have trolleys, but a table or box displayed with props, or a piece of wood or material with the equipment set out, can be a perfectly acceptable way to display resources. Children will need resources which are

Figure 5.1 A
resource trolley
for play outside.

positioned outside for easy access, but equally children will be free to move resources
and furniture between the outdoor and indoor areas.

Central to the planning of the physical environment is making sure there are enough
resources at hand, just in case more children become involved in a play setting than
was anticipated. There always seem to be enough pencils for children and they are not
expected to share, but this does not occur with all materials. In the McLean (1991) study
of Australian preschool teachers at work, she highlights one teacher who made sure
she had plenty of resources initially and as the day progressed made sure that if conflict
began over resources then either more were brought in or children were directed to
other equally relevant and often associated activities. Another teacher provided lots of
materials and open-ended activities and as a consequence children were cooperative
and 'frequently worked together on projects' (p. 68). As McLean argues, scarcity of
resources can so easily lead to peer conflict. The non-productive behaviour of another
setting where there are not so many resources could have been lessened had the
children had a wider choice and more interesting selection of materials to use (p. 133).

Interestingly, she discusses the work of Lindberg and Swedlow (1985) who state: 'An
understanding of sharing cannot be legislated suddenly; it must be developed in an
environment where a child feels that many things that he needs will be available to
him, although he cannot have everything he wishes' (p. 220). This would seem to be a
helpful suggestion for those who want to teach children that they have to learn to
share, and avoid situations which result in the survival of the fittest!

Which resources that are grouped together can have an effect on children's play and
subsequent learning? Nash (1981) considered that children associated equipment and
materials. If they were close by, children considered they could be used together. So in
the spatially-structured class, children used materials together in the creative area,
including dough, threaded beadwork, rocks, wood, box structures, collage materials
and paint. In the randomly-arranged class, children painted on paper and did not

combine materials. In this way children could only follow what was dictated, but in the structured class they could follow their own interest and so develop their imaginations. What is grouped within a bay, therefore, will affect what the children do. Carefully and clearly arranged resources will also affect play. Teets (1985) found that where art materials, dramatic materials and manipulative materials were displayed systematically and children could see how the materials were categorised, they made much better use of them. It follows, then, that if good quality play is sought there needs to be a sufficiency and variety of good quality resources which need to be well arranged. In well-resourced outdoor play areas, good equipment is used.

Resources can be gathered from a number of sources or they can be hand-made. For example, cloaks can be made from a piece of light material attached to a length of elastic, or firecrew breathing apparatus from a lemonade bottle and plastic tubing, with a mask made from a sleeping eye cover, and then strapped round the child's middle using a belt. Or materials can be gathered from charity shops and jumble sales; for example, bags and suitcases. Children also need to use real materials and tools, such as real hammers, trowels, money, cups, bowls and utensils. Families may also be willing to gather materials, and most importantly, children can make resources beforehand or as they go along and in this way take part ownership and part responsibility for the resources.

Boundaries

Given the nature of the outdoors, the learning bays cannot be permanent fixtures, and will have to be almost entirely cleared away each day. However, it is important that the particular areas for learning are carefully set up and each learning bay is divided from the others. Research by Teets (1985) into the relationship between environment and behaviour in day-care centres found that where boundaries to learning centres were set up, the number of interruptions was reduced. By virtue of having defined learning areas there was a reduction in the loss and misuse of equipment. Division does not mean, however, that the structure is permanent; it may be that the positioning of equipment will be sufficient division, or simply the clustering of some resources in one location will give a clear division. Or the learning areas can be divided by the resource trolley, box or table, similar to indoors. A simple chalkline on the ground can indicate to children that a particular area is for a particular activity.

As discussed in the previous chapter, too much permanent division of the garden can hinder children's learning, so any fixed hedging or trellising has to be really needed. Children can also be encouraged to use their own sense, be aware of others at work and know that they cannot go charging across an area with trucks where children are attempting to play bat-and-ball-games. In fact, the games children play will create their own boundaries. If children are given a chance to develop and extend, for example, their small-ball skills there will be no need to control excited kicking and throwing of balls, as the skill training will control the play. Boundaries need to be flexible and reflect the current play activities of each particular class. Alongside this will be the agreed rules, agreed between staff and children so that everyone knows that care has to be taken.

Continuity of provision

One of the difficulties with outdoor play is that equipment in most establishments has to be put away at the end of the day, whereas the indoor equipment can be left out. However, to ensure that children are able to follow their current interests and follow through ideas not fully formed, it is important to set up outdoors with some degree of continuity. Indoors, the planning will involve deciding daily what particular resources will be placed in each bay. The arrangement of resources acts as starting points for children's play. Sometimes it will be appropriate to leave the resources in the trolley for the children to start with a clean slate and sometimes it will be necessary to set up where they left off the day before. A learning bay such as the imaginative area needs to be available all of the time. However, it will be given a different identity as needs arise, for example, a pirate ship or rocket.

McLean (1991) describes ongoing play scenes, including the 'Telecom boys' where children were playing daily using various props which included ladders, shovels, a very thick rope, a hard hat, discarded telephone equipment and porters' trolleys. Another group were digging up a 'mine' and the boys liked to play for some time each day at this digging. The author describes the play as 'productive and highly elaborated as they unearthed interesting rocks and other long-lost (and sometimes recently-buried) objects' (p. 167). What a celebration of play this is! Children knew that the play they started one day could be carried on the next day and it would not be put away or broken up.

Similarly, experiments that children get involved in, such as those using water, need to be out for more than one day so that children have plenty of opportunities to explore the material. Lally (1991) reports that teachers find that where children are able to follow an interest over a period of time there is a great increase in motivation and concentration. Children need plenty of opportunities to use and modify the activities.

Imaginative play area

The first learning bay, and probably most important area to consider, is the imaginative play area. This will need resources which suit many possible permutations of play, whether it involves being a post lady, dog catcher, plasterer, TV repair person, zoo keeper, astronaut or pirate. It should enable children to work cooperatively, to negotiate, share, discuss, contemplate and conclude; it needs to be available on a daily basis in the same way as the imaginative play area would be inside. The difference with this outdoors fantasy area is that there is much more scope for movement and the play can be on a larger scale and involve the whole child.

This is the particular relevance of play – that it can be on a large scale and socio-dramatic. It means that children can use wheeled toys, which can be involved in the imaginative play of being, for example, milkmen, removal men, or a family. Children need equipment which can hold just one child, a number of children at a time, or materials. Children need trucks, hay carts, wooden pushchairs, carts, scooter carts, wheelbarrows. The important criteria when buying are that it has to be well-made and sturdy. Such items can be used in conjunction with bikes by simply tying the two together.

Much of the equipment associated with this play will also be relevant to the building and material play area. The larger items will include blocks, wooden and plastic crates, large cubes, A-Frames, climbing frames, planks, barrels, drums, large cardboard boxes, industrial tubing, tyres and treetrunk sections. Children can then use their combined imaginations to design what they wish or staff may set up an initial arrangement to spark ideas. The equipment used here is more versatile than, for example, the play cooker or sink as it allows children to use their imagination to make these be whatever they and the staff want them to be.

Other equipment could include large pieces of material, pieces of carpet, ladders, tents, various sized pieces of wood, large umbrellas. This area also needs chairs and possibly a table as children and staff need somewhere to sit in play settings and it is not always appropriate to sit on a crate or treetrunk section! Not all of this equipment should necessarily be put out all at once, but children do need to know that if they want a particular piece of equipment it can be made available. What is available, and how it is laid out, act as the starting points for a play setting, which children can add to and change.

There should also be a trolley with a host of props, such as clothes, accessories such as bags and hats, belts, sunglasses, hard hats, police hats, suitcases, baskets, backpacks. Tools such as firefighter breathing apparatus (home-made), tubing made into fire hoses, doctor's equipment and bag, tool belts, paint brushes, shovels, small spades, old cameras, telephones, personal stereos, binoculars, pulleys, mallets, home-made stretchers, containers, such as sweet jars or flower pots, pegs, sweeping brushes. The equipment does not have to be expensive; a makeshift tent from a piece of material, cooking utensils, sleeping bags made from material or a blanket, backpacks, a primus stove made by the children from recycled materials, sticks from the natural material collection to make a pretend fire, together have the makings of an effective camping playscene. Utensils from the kitchen could include the usual plates, saucepans, spoons, forks and so on. Dolls and clothing and bedding also need to be provided. Ropes can be used in a play setting and along with string, masking tape and elastic bands are the outdoors equivalent to making, adapting and sticking materials indoors, which include adhesive tape and glue. Rope/string, masking tape and elastic bands are so useful for outdoor play. One can throw a piece of material over an A-frame and keep it in place with string; it then becomes an immediate den or house. Masking tape can be used to attach signs to wooden, metal, plastic equipment. It will not stay in place forever but should stay long enough for the play scene. Ropes can be used to attach trucks to bikes, to hold boxes together in a truck. Looking to the Guiding Principles children can only control and modify their environment if they have the tools to do so. Clipboards with paper and pencils attached or white boards are writing materials which can be used in most weather. Number plates, home-made cones and road signs can add to the list of imaginative play materials. The list is almost endless, but has to not only reflect the experiences of the children but also offer new experiences.

Just as indoors we might change the focus of the imaginative area, so too we need to do this outdoors and, for example, set up a café, a pirate's ship, a fishing boat, a spaceship, dinosaur land. Again, props are needed to extend the play, extra to those already available. Children could be involved in the making of such materials: fishing rods for the boat, patches for the pirate ship, large trees for the dinosaur land. However, as already suggested, it is important to keep an imaginative area available for some time, just as we would indoors, otherwise children cannot extend any ideas from the day before, cannot continue work from the previous day and cannot build on skills learnt the day before, such as negotiation, collaboration and so on. So although much of the equipment will be made available daily for children to use, there will need to be a set-up play area left for a period of time. In this way there can be a number of play situations going on alongside each other.

Children need to know that if they wish, they can set up a fantasy or imaginative scene themselves and have available whatever props and resources they require. There always needs to be a balance between giving a focus to some, particularly those who may not have been taught how to play and giving a freedom to those who want too follow an interest. Some children do seem to have a real flare and almost insatiable need for imaginative play.

Bikes

Given the limited resources in school, bikes are possibly not the most important piece of equipment to buy as they can sometimes be more trouble than they are worth! I suggest that some teachers' fear of nursery education and outdoor play stems from what they have seen in poorly run settings – many children racing around a small area on bikes and scooters. This is not what quality Foundation Stage education is about. Some schools have made the decision not to have bikes or only to have bikes with attachments, so that social play is fostered. This has to be an issue discussed between staff. They can be dangerous and can become a source of power and ultimately disagreements. (See Chapter 7 – section 'Joining in with children's play'.) It can be frightening for adults, let alone children to have bikes being ridden about in a small area. It is difficult to foster cooperative play on a bike. However, the actual skill involved with riding a bike is relevant and it does give a great sense of achievement. In some areas children do not have access to places where they can ride safely. So, whether you have bikes or not has to be weighed up carefully, based on the needs of the children, space available and current resources. It may be that solitary bike riding has to be set up as an activity in the primary playground away from other play. Or it could be that there will be only two-wheeled bikes available in this area and so only a limited number of children will be able to use them.

Building, construction and material play area

Children need opportunities to build and use materials, which enable them to explore current concerns with regard to basic mathematical and scientific concepts. They need to be able to use, design, build and adapt. In this area children need opportunities to work together for a common goal, as in this way children learn to cooperate and get on to achieve the end product. It may be working together to build a tower using wooden offcuts and mud, or building a bridge using crates and planks. It may be that some of the children's play will move into the fantasy area, move out again and so on. Equipment such as cubes, plastic milk and bread crates, planks, cable spools, ladders can all be used for construction; so too ropes, plastic tubing, guttering and hose pipe. Essential items are wooden blocks, both hollow and ordinary, but these are expensive and need to be treated with care. If you are concerned about the impact of tarmac on the wood, using gym mats, pieces of carpet or material can help to prevent damage, but it will then be more difficult to build on.

Water and sand play can be part of this learning bay and can indeed be a mini-environment within the overall learning bay. Water play can be on a grander scale

Figure 5.2 Controlling the environment. These children were given plenty of oportunities to play with guttering and crates, to move water from one place to another. Children were able to set up and change the resources as they wished. They needed to negotiate to achieve a common goal.

outside and can incorporate guttering, a number of trays, long pieces of tubing and a plethora of buckets, thereby involving children in corporate activity. In this situation children have to work together, otherwise the play will not be fruitful. Cardboard boxes and plastic boxes and bricks can also be used, as too can a collection of sanded wood offcuts. Buckets and other containers can be used in this area.

And there is no reason why young children cannot use real tools, such as mallets, hammers and the like. A nursery school, highlighted in an article in *The Times Educational Supplement*, uses real tools and was commended by an OFSTED inspection (Klein 1997). Carpet and material or large pieces of cardboard can be a warmer and friendlier surface to work on during cold and damp weather. Such items will get wet and dirty and can be thrown away when they become too knocked about.

Natural materials can be used in conjunction with this area and imaginative play. Many of these could be stored outside, as they are not damaged by the weather and are unlikely to be stolen! Collections of stones, shells, twigs, seeds, leaves, bark, cork, bottle tops, pieces of wood, pebbles, gravel can be housed in containers which will not be blown over. These materials can be used in a variety of ways. They can be materials for imaginative play, or they can be materials for making discoveries about density, weight, volume. They may also be used to examine, draw and discuss as materials in

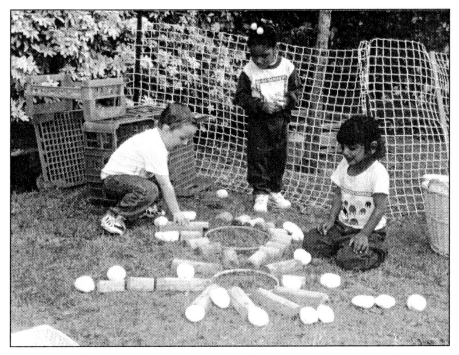

Figure 5.3 Making patterns using stones and half logs from a garden centre, plus embroidery rings.

their own right. These materials can be placed by the imaginative play bay, the building area, the scientific discovery area, or may be placed so they can be accessed for any play. It is also important to tell the children that they can access these materials whenever they wish.

Within this section there needs to be a digging patch, separate from the horticultural area. This would be for building and construction work, where children might simply want to see if they could build a structure using mud and bricks and wood, or it could be for imaginative play, where children might be tunnellers or be burying treasure. Resources here would include spades with strong shafts, trowels and the natural materials described above. When it is dry, children can sit on the ground and dig. Even on a damp, wet day children can still use this area without getting wet clothes by laying down large thick pieces of card or material on the grass or soil for children to kneel and sit on.

The gymnasium

The gymnasium learning bay is essentially about physical activity and developing physical skills and abilities, such as balance, coordination, climbing, swinging and strength. Children need to practise and modify their movements in order to reach a mature pattern of movement, but also to reach a high level of self-confidence. Once again, many of the resources used in the imaginative and building learning bays can be

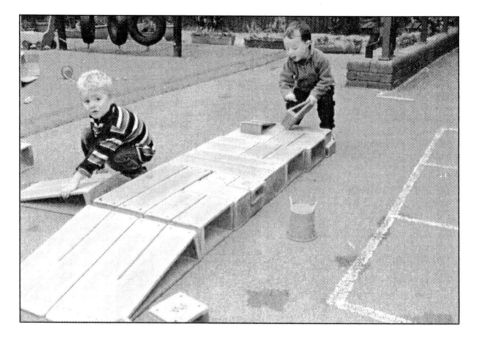

Figure 5.4 Building together outside.

used in the gymnasium learning bay. It may be that imaginative play will move into physical play and into building play. An A-frame or cube for climbing may then become a hiding place from a terrible monster! Children moving over stepping stones may be keeping safe from crocodiles. When separating out this area, it is very important to remember that movement occurs in all children's pursuits and not just in the gymnasium area. So much of outdoor play is about learning through movement.

Equipment needs to be set up for climbing, balancing, holding on with hands or legs, for stepping, for manoeuvring around. Planks, slides, ladders, nesting bridges or A-frames, boxes, crates, barrels, tunnels are examples of equipment for this area. They can be arranged on different levels, at various angles, connected together to create slides, walkways, bridges, stepping stones. For example, there could be an arrangement of balance bars and A-frames, followed by hoops to jump or step into, boxes to step onto and off, ladders attached to the top of A-frames for children to hang from. Strengthening arm muscles is very important at this stage for the eventual development of finer muscles. Treetrunk sections, carpet squares and tyres can act as stepping stones. Cones or boxes can be arranged in intervals for running in and out of. Canes across crates can act as jumping poles or for manoeuvring under.

These kinds of obstacle courses are for children to work at alone or together, but they are for children to use to practise and develop their own skills at their own pace. Children can attempt whatever part of the gymnasium they wish, dependent on their confidence and readiness. A plank attached to an A-frame, for example, can be set lower or higher depending on the child. The gymnasium can be laid out in a circle or in a line; there can be two gymnasiums set up, or the focus can be on vigorous activity: it can be a running course, with cones to weave in and out of, boxes to climb onto and jump off and lines to jump over. The set-up obviously has to reflect the needs of the particular group of children.

The concentration involved in physical activity can be intense, but the children will set the pace, challenge and speed, and staff can also offer challenges which will enable each child to develop and try something new, in a different way or simply to go faster. Staff can give guidance, support and encouragement. Staff can also use such an activity to enable children to use and feel such words as 'through', 'underneath', 'over', 'into' and many other prepositions. Again, this area can be changed and adapted as a session progresses. So, although staff may set up an arrangement at the beginning of the session, children may rearrange it as they wish. Children will work carefully together to set up a new arrangement, and can in fact be asked to set the arrangement up at the start of the session for others to use.

It may be that there is a scarcity of equipment, or only a small garden. However, if physical development is considered to be important then it needs to be provided for in some way. Ropes laid on the ground can act as a balancing bar, planks of wood on the ground can be used for balancing. A ladder straddled across two large wooden boxes can be used for manoeuvring across (as long as staff are holding it in place) and even underneath for children to take their weight on their arms, with their legs lifted. This is not ideal, but is one way round a lack of equipment. A lack of outdoor space may mean that a gymnasium could be set up in the infant playground. Again this is not ideal, but possibly the only solution, or it could be set up inside. Whatever can be provided, children need opportunities to develop their skills and confidence over time. Bruce (1987) argues that if children only experience an activity periodically they cannot build up skills.

Setting up the gymnasium is a starting point with regard to developing movement skills. Through observations of children, staff can assess how other activities are enabling children to develop physical skills. As McAuley and Jackson (1992) argue, when analysing the Hutt *et al.* (1989) research, combined physical and imaginative play can simply be overlooked; observers only see physical activity or imaginative play and do not see how the two are combined. The importance of outdoor play is that the play is at a physical level because children are using their whole bodies. This is not about playing with small doll's house figures, or standing to paint a picture, this is about being a milk deliverer, telephone repair man, a street player. The whole body is used and physical skills are developed. When children are combining physical and fantasy play they need to be safe and be aware of what makes them safe and what does not.

Horticultural area

Through this particular learning bay children are learning scientific and environmental concepts; they can also be learning a good deal more with regard to care and support. This learning bay is always there and does not need to be taken indoors. But if using tubs and pots, and the school is in an area where vandalism occurs, it may be necessary to move such equipment inside. However, the ideal would be a plot of land in which children can plant, tend and harvest flowers and vegetables. If this is not possible or available then wooden boxes, tubs, plant pots, growbags, in fact any container, such as a washing up bowl, a bucket or an old tyre could be used to put plants in. Wooden or brick tubs set at the child's level are particularly effective and enable children to plant, tend and observe easily.

The very important aspect of this activity is the fact that something develops and

Figure 5.5 A gymnasium arrangement, put together by children and staff.

changes over time, which can then be recorded, so a camera is an essential item. Children can make their own books or joint books to record what they did and what happened. It means that children who prefer to work outside can be involved with writing, drawing, graph-making and so on, which they may not do so readily inside.

This learning bay would benefit from some form of boundary, such as a low fence, a section of grass or a layer of bricks or pebbles so that children know this area cannot be used for play purposes. Initially this would probably have to be an area where children and staff work together. As the children grow in knowledge and confidence they could be allowed to weed and water without too much supervision.

Resources in this area could include child-sized spades, trowels, forks, hoes, watering cans, hoses, canes, wheelbarrows together with the necessary seeds and plants. This area can easily be organised into two cycles, one which progresses from September to April and one which starts in April and carries through to September.

You do not have to be an experienced gardener. You may not be able to display in the local flower and produce show, but the fruit and vegetables will be of a sufficient size for children to see their growth and appreciate them; crucial is to see the cycle through. It is also important to think about when the harvest is due, otherwise children who leave at the end of the term may miss the cycle of events. Children need to appreciate the life cycle and to record it, in words, drawings, photos, collage, paint and any other medium possible. A herb garden or tub can be a most effective way of introducing children to smell comparisons. (See Cooper and Johnson (1991) to check poisonous plants.)

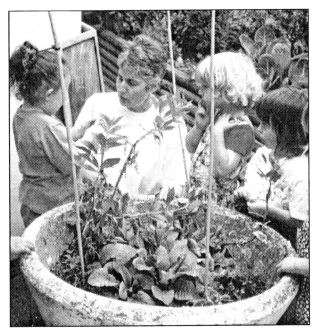

Figure 5.6 Adults and children working together.

Environment and science bay

This can consist of old rotten logs or a piece of carpet which is left in a damp, secluded spot for the gathering of mini-beasts. This can be lifted periodically for the investigation and observation of such creatures. An old sink or bathtub can provide a habitat for water-keen mini-beasts, but beware that open water will attract mosquitoes. Resources connected with this learning bay and which need to be readily available on a trolley, or in clearly labelled boxes, will be inspection pots, magnifying glasses, gathering jars, pond-dipping equipment, paper and pencils on clipboards so that children can record what they are seeing.

Figure 5.7 Some plants for growing in the horticultural area

For the spring:
daffodils, crocuses, snowdrops, tulips.

For the summer/autumn:
    hardy annuals such as alyssum, asperula, candytuft, clarkia, clary, lavatera, limnanthes, nasturtium, scabious, virginian stock, for an excellent display of colour, shape and texture;
    anemones, freesia, iris and liatris spicata;
    beans, carrots, marrows, potatoes (also the early variety), tomatoes;
    cosmos, marigolds, petunias.

For the winter:
    Purple sprouting broccoli for harvesting the following year.

A clear link with an indoor learning bay can be seen here: children will need reference books so they can identify and learn about the various creatures and these can be easily displayed in the book corner. Books can be made by staff which specifically identify the organisms the children are looking for and, likewise, children and staff can make reference books for everyone to use. Again, the camera needs to be close at hand to record interesting sightings – if possible a Polaroid; not only does this provide a historical record but it does so immediately. There is also the potential to have bird tables, bird boxes and baths. If situated near a class window, when the children are not outside they will be able to observe the birds. Together with the resources already mentioned, other ideas include bought and home-made kites, bubble blowers and bubbles, a wormery, calibrated containers for the collection of snow, to allow the children to record the change in volume or to collect rain to see how much has fallen in a given time, pin-wheels and so on. Ouvry (2000) suggests putting together something called 'weather boxes' (p. 70). These are activities, resources, books, pictures, songs and poems all ready to be used if that particular weather feature occurs, whether it be wind, rain, snow or sun. This seems a great idea, as children need to have multi-sensory experience of these weather features – not be stuck inside looking at it! But for the experience to be really worthwhile it is very effective to have the ideas and resources at the ready. So for example Ouvry suggests covering umbrellas with different materials ready to explore the different sound rain makes on different materials. She suggests putting a drop of oil on a puddle, followed by a discussion about colour and rainbows. Another idea is dressing two dolls, one in a rainproof material, one in woolly material, leaving in the rain and following up with discussions. These boxes could be added to, with ideas that children come up with and as more ideas are found.

Small apparatus area

Outside is the ideal place for children to practise and refine small motor skills, as there is space to use equipment, without anything getting damaged. Again, children need regular access to small apparatus, otherwise skills cannot be refined. If children are only offered opportunities to use balls periodically then skills cannot be built upon. A resource trolley with balls of various sizes, and hoops, quoits, beanbags, skipping ropes, bats, skittles is needed. It needs to be positioned as far away from other activities as feasible. It may only be possible to have a few balls used at one time because games can become too chaotic with lots of balls going wide of the mark.

Again, if the space available is limited then a small group could be taken to the primary playground or primary hall, or less bouncy balls, or beanbags or the equivalent may have to be used. Although it is fun to throw wildly, children should be encouraged to throw carefully; throwing *to* someone, *into* something, *through* something, *at* something. A small game of throwing into a bowl or bucket can be set up, or a chalked target can be marked out on the ground or wall. Children can be encouraged to kick or bat a ball into a receptacle, at the wall or over a line. A simple grid with the numbers 1 to 10 can be chalked on the ground for children to aim at and staff can encourage children to throw at the number 5, number 7 and so on. Likewise, letters, names or words can be chalked on the ground to aim at, thereby developing reading skills alongside motor skills.

Figure 5.8 A water wheel.

Quiet bay

Indoors there are quiet spots for reflection, or for doing activities which require little movement; such spots are also needed outdoors. A table and chairs in a shaded or cosy spot would be preferable, but seats from indoors or a couple of crates would be fine, and so too would a blanket, a piece of carpet plus cushions. However arranged, children must be aware that this is a quiet spot. A proper wooden seat enclosed either with a pergola or surrounded by shrubs would be useful, as this can act as shade in the summer and a windbreak in the winter. Even in the smallest outdoor area, a quiet spot can be established. A box with books, tape recorder, soft toys, paper and pencils, language and mathematics games can be set up here.

Visual representation is central to young children, whether it be drawing, painting or making a design from blocks. Therefore, outside drawing materials need to be available everyday. Matthews (1994) demonstrates how young children can put drawing and letters together to 'make free-flowing associations and multiple meanings' (p. 93). He goes further in describing a particular picture, to ponder on whether it is the beginning of making puns and could indicate a child thinking about thinking, representing to reflect upon representation. This is higher order thinking and needs to flourish.

It is not always possible to set up outdoors as picturesquely as indoors, but it is still important to provide this spot. At other times, a board game, a threading activity, books on a particular topic can be offered. In this way those children who are reticent about venturing outdoors have a secure spot to go to, while those who work

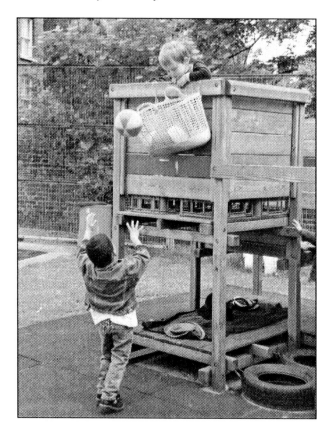

Figure 5.9 Getting the ball in the basket.

confidently outdoors but need time to have a quiet and settled period are also provided for. Any child who wishes just to watch what is happening outside is also catered for. It also means that those children who are not confident about the more formal aspects of school work, can have a go in an environment in which they feel secure.

Other areas for learning

The learning bays mentioned previously are but the beginning, and ensure that there is a balance of activities available. But what is offered outside does not have to end there and other activities and learning areas can be set up. Painting can, of course, be provided outside, but it is best when it is not windy. Outdoors provides the perfect spot for foot printing, as the mess created does not cause the same problems for clearing up as it does indoors. Some children may prefer to use chalks outside on the ground to create pictures and writing. Group painting on a large piece of paper taped to a wall can be effective in encouraging reticent painters. Clay, a natural material which is not used as much as it should be, can be set up more easily outdoors, as any difficulties with mess are not as much a problem outdoors as indoors. A music corner can mean that children can really make sounds without disturbing anyone. A music table, with instruments and resources used in a group music session, will enable children to practise and try out ideas from the music session. Group reading, music, dance, movement, snacks, meals can all be offered outside, and in this way the outdoor area becomes the outdoor classroom. It may be that the woodwork table can be put outside. Interestingly, in one school the woodwork table outside created an unnecessary diversion and staff felt it was better placed just inside the door along with all other design materials. As with our provision for inside, what we can and do provide outside is dependent to a large extent on the imagination of the staff.

Resources and equipment

I have always been reticent about providing a list of resources and equipment as I worry that it will be seen as definitive. However, having been asked so many times for a list I do so with this caution. This is just a list of the basics that could be provided in a Foundation Stage outdoor area. It does not contain any fixed equipment, nor bikes. What is provided under the heading 'imaginative play' is as long as one's imagination! The most expensive pieces of equipment will be the blocks, A-frames, trucks. Some equipment will be free, for example the material or carpet. Some equipment can be multi-purpose, for example a skipping rope. This can be used to skip with alone or as a jumping over/going under game. It can be used to tie a truck to a bike, or to keep some crates secure in a truck. It can be placed straight on the ground and used to balance along. Letter or number shapes can be made with it. A den can be made by securing material with a rope over an A-frame or cubes. Really the list of possible uses for this one item is endless and it does not cost a fortune. Many of the items mentioned are multi-purpose.

Please do read this list in conjunction with the main text.

A frames/folding trestles – large and small
Wooden planks – small and large
Metal ladders
Child-sized wooden ladders
Play-cubes
Milk and bread crates, or some sort of box for building, strong enough for a child to stand on
Hollow blocks and unit blocks
Pull-along trucks/trailers
Imaginative play equipment, including dressing-up clothes and accessories
Masking tape, elastic bands, string/rope (these are the equivalent of indoor making and sticking materials)
Large pieces of material
Pieces of carpet, carpet squares
Folding climbing frame
Hoops and skipping ropes (without hard ends)
Tubing and guttering, plus a host of water and sand equipment
Chairs or seating of some sort
Balls and bats – various sizes
Drawing materials
Writing, reading and mathematical games and materials
Trolleys to hold equipment

'Weather boxes'
Tree-trunk sections
Mini-beast resource box
Gardening tools and resource box
Reclaimed equipment, such as cardboard boxes, card tubing, spools.

Together, the companies listed in the Useful contacts section at the back of this book supply the equipment – no one company supplies everything. The 'boxes' mentioned cannot be bought, but will be put together by the staff.

In conclusion

Learning bays are starting points: they help children to get started in their play, they give a focus which they may or may not follow. The bays help to make sure a broad and balanced curriculum is offered and that no important component is left out. The bays need to be seen by everyone as flexible and play needs to be allowed to move freely across the combined environments of indoors and outdoors; similarly it has to be allowed to progress from one bay to another.

Figure 5.10 (opposite) gives some idea of what an outdoor area might look like. There are seven bays arranged:
Imaginative – which is a supermarket delivery depot, with trucks, large cardboard boxes, cones, plank and tables with a large number of different containers from shops. Children have chalk-drawn a road.
Construction – partially arranged by the staff, but children to build as they wish. Also a digging plot with tools – large hole made.
Gymnasium – A-frames, planks, crates, barrel, mats, log sections, carpet squares.
Small apparatus – trolley with various sized bats, balls, hoops, ropes. Chalks to mark out targets.
Horticulture – tools, outside tap. Plants in various stages of development, seeds to be put in.
Quiet area – chairs, cushions, carpet squares. Tree for shade. Books, drawing pads, tapes, games.
Mini-beast area – log, carpet squares, tree trunk. Cardboard squares for stepping stones.
Shed – children can easily access more resources as shed is well arranged and labelled. By class wall a collection of stones, pebbles and wood for use in any play.

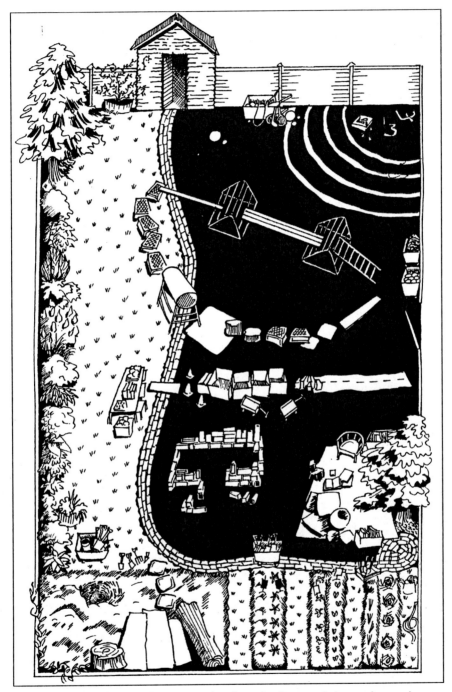

Figure 5.10 A possible outdoor layout, showing mixed areas of play, surface and content. (Prepared by Sue Coffey, 2002)

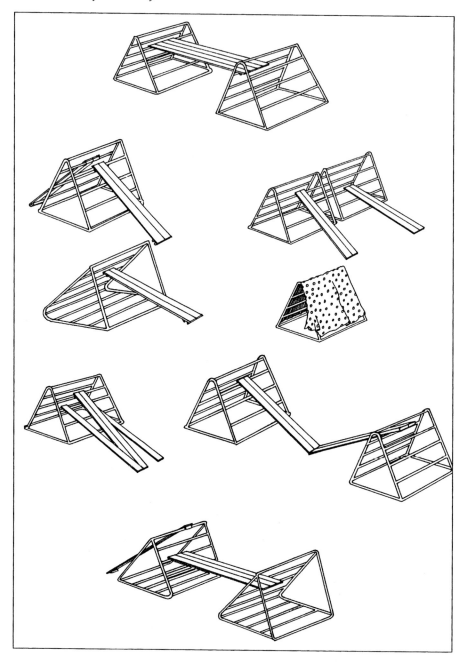

Figure 5.11 A-frames, planks and material in various arrangements. (Prepared by Sue Coffey, 2002)

6: Children using the outdoor environment

Sometime ago when I was supervising students on teaching practice two students observed marked changes in children's behaviour when they went outdoors to play. The students were working in nurseries in different catchment areas where the approaches of the staff were different, and both had a set playtime. One child was an able boy who could concentrate and persevere at activities. Inside the nursery he was shy and reserved but when he went outdoors he became much more outgoing and confident in his approach and in the use of equipment. The student commented that he was almost two children. The other child was a girl, who when outdoors would enter into imaginative games with other children, including mother and baby scenarios, horse riding games and house parties, all based around the outdoor play house. However, inside the classroom she rarely played or chatted to other children but tended to involve herself in adult-controlled activities, even though there was a well-stocked home corner, which was set away from the main part of the nursery. Again, the student commented that the girl was giving off quite different messages about herself in the two environments. The two children became more confident outdoors, and more keen to play with other children. It could be that the children had 'read' the adult expectations of indoors as being quiet and busy, and that outdoors the children felt that they controlled the territory more and they therefore felt freer to express themselves; or it could be that the open space, the freedom or the ability to get away from adults, as in the case of the outdoor play house, was the trigger that changed their behaviour. Playing with other children may have been frowned upon indoors but expected outdoors. That is not to say that the adults expressed these ideas explicitly, but they were conveyed implicitly and as children want to please others and to be accepted and praised, they will try to fit in with the 'system'.

Children's behaviour is affected by many things: the weather, the type of morning the family has had before arriving at school, hunger, tiredness, illness, worries, but, as shown throughout this book, the environment also has an effect. As discussed earlier, evidence has shown that:

- overcrowding can affect children and cause aggression,
- being given uninterrupted time to work will encourage children to persevere more,
- in big open spaces children can feel lost, and
- timetabling can cause a number of behaviour problems.

It is evident that only some children succeed at school and that some children enjoy school more than others. How well a child gets on in school will have something to do with the person, as well as the actual school, teacher, and any number of other factors. How children do may also be based on gender. In this book we have been considering how one particular environment, the outdoors, can be organised to be an effective teaching and learning environment for all children. However, it may be that some groups of children would do better at school if they were able to play, learn and be taught in an environment in which they feel secure and happy, in a place that is natural for them to learn in.

The aim of this chapter is to:

- compare the play of children indoors and outdoors,
- look at the underachievement of boys,
- look at the way in which girls are unable to access some aspects of play,
- look at a case study of a partially-sighted child using the outdoor environment,
- see how the curriculum could be made more accessible to these children by bringing it to them, as opposed to their having to seek it out.

Comparing play indoors and outdoors

Tizard *et al.* (1976b), looking into four-year-olds' play in preschool centres, found striking differences in preference for outdoor play between working class and middle class children, with the working class choosing to spend 75 per cent of their time outside. The authors noted that the play of the working class children outdoors was more mature and they talked more than when indoors, where these children tended to be on their own more, games were shorter and less complex and social play was less advanced. If the working class children had only been observed indoors then their play would have appeared less mature than they were capable of. Cooperative group play was more likely to be found outdoors and contact between adult and child and non-social play with creative materials more likely indoors. In conclusion, the authors found that the working class children were removing themselves from the educational intentions of the staff.

Henniger (1985), looking into preschool children's behaviour in the indoor and outdoor settings, concluded that the indoor environment may inhibit some children socially. He found that the dramatic play of boys and older children was strongly influenced by the outdoor environment where both groups engaged in more play of this type. Henniger also found that cooperative play, the highest level of social play, was observed in nearly equal amounts indoors and outdoors. He felt that the lack of significant difference between the amount of cooperative play indoors and outdoors was important, as some children can be inhibited by being indoors, because of the limitations of space, floor covering and allowable noise levels. These factors may prevent the more active types of play which encourage boys to engage in the higher levels of social play. The only significant difference was that the younger children preferred cooperative play indoors.

A study by Whitehurst (2001) into her own practice found that pretend play was the most dominant form of play outside and that personal, social, emotional development was very much in evidence outside. Social skills and self-esteem were in greatest evidence followed by enthusiasm for learning, attention and persistence. The author makes a clear link between play and personal, social and emotional development, arguing that play contributes to this aspect of learning. However, she further argues that for this to happen children need to be able to access the area independently, have time to play and have resources freely available.

The Northern Illinois University research into visual–motor integration found that children's behaviour indoors was different from that of children working outdoors. Children working outdoors became 'strikingly assertive and imaginative' (Yerkes 1982, p. 4). Hutt *et al.* (1989) found that boys spent more time than girls outdoors on physical play and girls spent more time on material play. The activity span for boys was slightly longer than for girls when outdoors and boys tended to exhibit the longest activity spans in physical play outdoors; for girls the highest activity span was on material play indoors. From this research it would appear that:

- some children prefer to play in the outdoor environment,
- for some the level of learning was higher when outdoors,
- some were less inhibited outdoors,
- some were more assertive,
- some concentrated longer.

Clearly, environment affects children in different ways and can give a different picture of a child, as demonstrated in the example of the two children at the start of this chapter. Outdoor play may suit some children more than others, but it may also give children the opportunity to be more assertive and thereby more inventive than indoors.

Why do boys underachieve in school?

There is now concern among early years experts that the National Curriculum and testing 'could breed a generation of super-girly girls and disaffected boys' (Parkin 1997, p. VI) and that in fact schools suit girls more than boys. Walkerdine (1996) argues that the reason girls show early success at school is that they take up the right 'positions in pedagogic discourses' (p. 300), while boys do not take part in this discourse: they stay silent, and do not take part in the domestic games which are being taught by those who are used to a domestic play setting. Even more concerning is Walkerdine's (1996) suggestion that boys clearly do not feel at home in domestic imaginative situations, as girls have the controlling hand. She found that boys wanted either to remove themselves from domestic play or change the play because they were subservient. Walkerdine further argues that boys rarely played dominant father roles when the girls were present, but did when they were playing only with boys.

Millard (1997) argues that reading is seen as an activity more appropriate to girls than boys and that boys and girls create different educational experiences for themselves. Boys create more discipline problems for teachers; they take more of the teachers' time and actively oppose teachers giving girls equal time and emphasise the negative aspects of female sexuality, all from an early age. Paley (1984) came to the conclusion, in her fascinating study of boys and girls in her classroom, that the curriculum she offered suited the girls better than the boys. She found that the girls would go to the table activities associated with 'work' much more readily, while the boys would avoid these activities. She talks about the fact that girls are at an advantage because they are able to achieve more quickly and easily than boys. So boys get easily discouraged from the work associated with the table activities, because they are concerned about failing. For girls, the work at the table is play, and they will use the equipment whether the teacher is there or not. The boys do not find it so easy and so they, having tried the table activities, go back to the blockplay and more vigorous imaginative play that is associated with being a superhero.

O'Sullivan (1997), commenting on research at Keele University, suggests that starting school earlier is bad news for boys who are not ready for more formal teaching, as their overwhelming need for emotional support and external approval is not being met. Further, Paley found that not receiving an immediate sense of achievement makes boys give up more quickly than girls. O'Sullivan discusses research which argues that boys are treated more often as part of a group and not individually, whereas girls are treated as individuals and this does not help boys in their overwhelming need for individual recognition. Boys' need for superhero play is not being met at school but, as Jordan (1995) describes, is perfectly normal behaviour for them. He describes boys' cooperative fantasy play as 'warrior discourse' and states that boys from the beginning of time have sought out these great heroes to follow, whether Hercules or Dirty Harry. Through this play, boys are making meaning as to what being a boy and man is about.

Tony Bertram argues that as boys are more lively and exploratory, school does not suit them as well as the girls who are quieter and willing to sit and learn and accept the formal atmosphere of school (Burstall 1997). The actual play boys choose tends to involve high levels of physical activity.

Even such a simple thing as space or lack of space may affect boys and girls differently. Research by Brian Bates into overcrowding in a playgroup suggests that it has differing affects on boys and girls (Bates 1996). He found that as the room became more crowded the boys became more aggressive and formed into groups while the girls became more isolated and played alone. He points to other research which argues the same points, that the more crowded a class became the more solitary the children became, but if they did interact, it was more aggressively. He concludes that children are affected in the short and long term by the conditions under which we teach them and by the methods. Environment *does* have an effect.

The part of the brain which controls spatial development is more developed in boys and the hemisphere which manages language is more developed in girls. In boys the bridge between the two hemispheres is underdeveloped when they are born. 'In a less information-led age, this mattered less: crudely put, boys could fix things and girls could talk. Nowadays, we have a feminised culture when talking IS fixing things' (Neumark 1997, p. 6). But there is more to this: girls and boys do appear to use different areas of the brain when reading; girls tend to activate both hemispheres and boys tend to activate only the left. Boys mature at a slower rate than girls, so when girls are ready to go to school, boys are often not.

Children have different learning styles; these can be visual (learn and remember images, shapes and colour), auditory (learn and remember voices, sounds and music), and kinaesthetic (learn and remember by doing, moving and by touching). Noble *et al.* (2001) argue that more boys than girls prefer the kinaesthetic style, but that 'English schools tend to put heavy stress on the other two styles' (p. 99). In this way boys are not able to access the curriculum through a style they find easy.

Language lies at the heart of learning and schooling, but in the early years boys often find it hard to make a good start on reading. Through the Leverhulme Primary Improvement Project at Exeter University, Wragg and his associates have found that boys start school four or five points behind girls in the NFER Reading Tests. And this level hardly changes by the end of the year. Teachers tend to be mostly female and find it easier to associate with girls and their interests. For example, Millard's (1997) study of children's literacy suggests that the narrative fiction most valued by teachers is that which is favoured by girls. Therefore, boys' interest in action and adventure is seen as a deficit model. Paley (1984) describes how she found it easier when boys were 'not being boys' but acting more like girls.

Schools for all

It is clear that boys as a group are not doing as well at school as girls, or as well as they could do (Wragg 1997). There seems to be a growing belief that the school system itself is as much to blame as other factors for this failing and that the school system is not able to adapt itself to the needs of boys. Where education should be able to fit the child, it would seem that the child is having to fit the system and if they are unable to do so they are likely to fail. The evidence does not suggest that all boys underachieve but that a large proportion of them do. Ted Wragg (1997) argues that tackling the underachievement of boys is a very important challenge for the future. His ten-point plan includes:

- ensuring that boys attend nurseries, so that they make an early start on language activities and learn to behave well in class;
- offering topics such as adventure, humour, sport in their reading matter; and
- helping them to stay on task.

Steve Biddulph, a family therapist, argues that schools should adapt to the needs of boys, given that boys develop at a different rate and in a different sequence from girls. He suggests that boys should not start school at the same time as girls, because they are not ready to do school work and be sedentary in their learning at the same time (Neumark 1997).

Millard (1997) argues that schools need to become more 'boy friendly' (p. 167) with regard to reading, but without affecting the practices which have helped girls. This would include making reading more accessible and appealing to boys. Bertam suggests that we should be providing education 'both gender' ways (Burstall 1997), and neither sex should be debarred from experiences they would not have in the normal course of things.

Paley (1984) considers that 'if Jack is allowed to climb the beanstalk first, there is a better chance he will seek out work the moment he comes down' (p. 106). She suggests that boys need to be given more chance to play and not spend time struggling at the work which girls actually see as play. She argues that lesson plans should go so that boys will realise that table work is table play. When Paley increased the amount of free playtime, interestingly enough the girls used the extra time to play in the doll corner and with the blocks, and the boys used the time to go to the tables. So, in fact, increased playtime encouraged the boys to venture to the work aspects of the class.

In terms of the Foundation Stage experience it would seem that the outdoor environment could play a central role in helping boys. Boys are more interested in movement, exploration and action and this type of activity occurs for the most part in the outdoor area. If more boys do prefer the kinaesthetic learning style, this does indeed involve doing, moving and touching. Noble *et al.* (2001) argue that 'some under-performing boys would do much better if they were given a richer, kinaesthetic learning diet' (p. 99). This type of learning style needs to be offered from the beginning of a child's school life.

By giving less attention to the quality of outdoor play, schools may be denying access of education to a major sector of the child population and starting the downward spiral for some children. It is therefore essential that quality outdoor play is offered. Offering the curriculum in an environment in which children feel secure means that children learn more easily and do not see this as an achieve/fail situation. But also the more formal aspects of the curriculum can be offered in this secure environment and boys will not be 'turned off' by it, as they will see the 'work' as play, as the girls in the Paley study did. This is a case of 'taking the curriculum to the child'. Given that the age of entry to school will not be changing in the foreseeable future, it is our duty to wrap the formal aspects of the curriculum in a mode of learning best suited to children. If they are still in a very movement-orientated mode, an exploratory 'climb-the-beanstalk' stage, then the curriculum can be offered through this movement mode. If boys are different from girls and learn in different ways and if we don't want a culture of disaffected boys then we will need to intervene and help.

Girls and outdoor play

Equality of opportunities suggests that all children have a right to equal access to all activities and people in the class. However, this is clearly not happening and, in particular, not outdoors.

In the blockplay research, Gura (1992) argues that, indeed, territory and dominance are linked and that boys dominated an area of the class environment, namely the blockplay area; a finding which also comes through in the Halliday *et al.* (1985) research from New Zealand. Hutt *et al.* (1989) found that boys were more competent and decisive in their choice of activities than girls. Tizard *et al.* (1976a) found that boys tended to dominate outdoor play and girls tended to play more with fixed equipment (climbing frames and swings), while boys tended to play more with the movable equipment (wheeled toys and larger constructional materials, such as crates, tyres and ladders). Cullen (1993) found that girls and boys used the outdoor area in different ways and that the differences followed stereotypes of girls' and boys' play found in other studies. The boys played with the more active equipment and the girls tended to stay with the quieter home-type play.

Hart (1978), in a study of sex differences in the use of outdoor space, found that boys tended to modify the landscape more frequently and more effectively than girls; when girls modified it, it was more often than not in their imaginations, so bushes became walls, lateral branches became shelves. When girls did get involved with building, it was with boys and it was the boys who organised it. Boys tended to build the outer parts of the building (walls, windows, roofs) and girls dealt with interior design. But particularly significant was the finding that when boys came across girls building, they would take over and the girls would become subservient. So there appears to be an unhealthy dominance, with girls taking on a lesser role.

A partially-sighted child using the outdoor area

DJ was a partially-sighted child with sickle cell anaemia who came to nursery just after he was four. His mother was concerned as to how he would fit into this environment with its bustle and activity. A teaching assistant was assigned to DJ and there was a teacher and nursery nurse for 26 children. The nursery operated so that indoors and outdoors were available simultaneously.

DJ could make out shapes and shades of things and tended to move about using this knowledge. Initially, DJ was very tentative and stayed close to an adult and needed, rather than a helping hand, helpful information about what was around him and a warning if he was going towards something he had not seen. DJ's favourite area was outdoors and he played outdoors every day for a good deal of the session. He found indoors frustrating as he bumped into tables and chairs, but outdoors he did not have

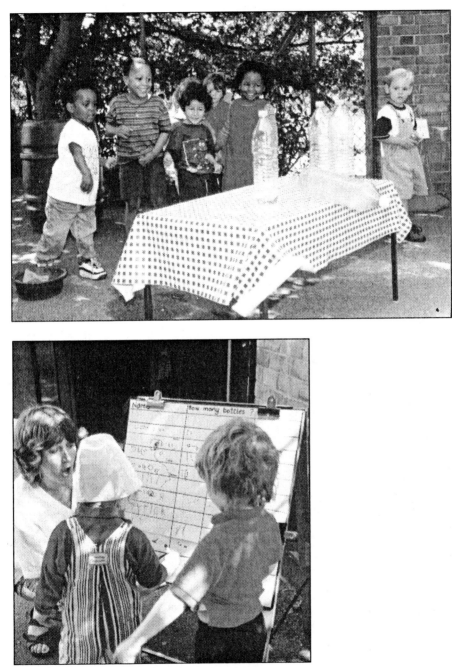

Figure 6.1 A skittles game and recording the score.

the same difficulties. This was interesting as the indoor space was very large and uncluttered. The difficulty he had outdoors was that the equipment tended not to be in exactly the same place every day and so the staff helped by telling him where the equipment was before he started to play.

Once DJ had settled into the nursery, he did not need to be told where the equipment was but simply stopped, looked and pinpointed the positions himself. In particular he enjoyed playing on the climbing frame when it was set up as an imaginative play situation. He not only played on the equipment, he also manoeuvred boxes, planks, barrels, and the like, to design, build and make himself. If he got into difficulties, for example getting a plank caught and not being able to see what was stopping it, he preferred not to be helped and often got quite upset if an adult intervened. DJ enjoyed climbing, he would use the gymnasium set-ups, and would be happy as long as he could go at his own pace. He could even run but never fast. He enjoyed working in the wild area, where insects were studied close-up. He could follow a ball but if something else crossed his path, he would often not see it and this is when bumps would occur. In terms of PE lessons in the Infant hall, DJ was initially supported by one member of staff who stayed close and gave helpful information. By and by, DJ did not need this help and got on with what was asked. He learnt to cope with children moving quickly about the hall, say, for example, when they were asked to run and change direction. He was helped in this because the other children were 'DJ-aware'; they knew that they had to be aware of him and not to run at him. But equally, DJ wanted to do whatever was on offer, and never said he could not do anything.

DJ had two illnesses which one could say made him unsuited to outdoor play but he needed and wanted to work outdoors. Outdoor play gave him a good deal of confidence, and laid the foundations for later learning. His mother was understandably very anxious and sometimes over-protective. Outdoor play gave him opportunities to do things that his mother would not have felt confident about him doing, but the staff in the nursery were able in a very supportive environment to give him the experiences that he needed. Outdoors also gave DJ a freedom of movement he could not find indoors. The importance of talking about DJ is that outdoor play is for everyone and any child should be able to access it.

Taking the curriculum to the children

As it appears that boys are not achieving as well as they should at school, it would seem that schools should be more 'boy friendly'. They need to consider doing it 'both gender ways' and may need to let Jack 'climb the beanstalk first'. It would also appear that failure at school starts early and that help and intervention need to start as soon as possible. Boys are very movement-orientated – they like to build and construct and they enjoy acting out and playing imaginative games with others. It would seem then that schools need to consider how to 'take the curriculum' to these children, as opposed to expecting them to access the curriculum as they are clearly not succeeding in this at present. It would seem that outdoors is a preferred place for boys and perhaps if the curriculum is taken to boys in this environment they may be able to access it more easily. This means that not only must Foundation Stage staff make outdoor play interesting, but they also must get more involved in the play and devise ways to fit the more formal components of the curriculum into this setting.

As educators we have a brief to ensure that everyone has equality of access to the whole curriculum. Girls are clearly not getting this equality, some activities are being denied them because of domination by boys, some activities are being denied because, as a group, girls tend to want adult presence.

Margaret McMillan considered that all children would benefit from nursery education but that they would all get different things from it. For example, the children from the affluent parts of Chelsea were nicknamed the Kensington Cripples by the middle class parents, who set up the Open Air Nursery in the 1930s, because they had everything done for them by servants and could do little for themselves (Whitbread 1972, p. 72). McMillan felt this group could benefit from simply doing things for themselves.

'Taking the curriculum to children' can simply mean having an adult present who participates in play, protecting children from others who may want to take over, and showing the potential of the material to those involved. But it also means giving the children confidence to use the materials. How adults can support children is discussed in greater detail in the next chapter.

Taking the curriculum to the children may simply mean moving activities, such as language and mathematical games, books and tapes, from indoors to outdoors. The presence of such activities outdoors, in what some children may feel is a less pressurised and freer atmosphere, may be the spark to enable children to use the materials. One particular child I remember in a nursery was very reticent about painting, gluing, digging and using sand and water. He was a child who enjoyed outdoor play and physical activity. Staff had tried various approaches to help him use these materials and then one day foot-printing was offered outside. He very eagerly took his socks and shoes off and got 'stuck into' the foot-printing. One cannot say that this experience caused him to start using paint, to dig or work in the sand but, coincidentally, it was after this experience that he started joining in with those activities.

Likewise, a teacher in a nursery class was concerned that a number of the girls seemed to be monopolising the home corner and a number of boys were controlling the block area. One evening she simply swapped the position of these two learning areas and the next day the boys went to the same place as before but discovered the home corner and the girls went to the same area and found the blocks. What was even more surprising was the way in which both groups took up roles appropriate to that area, with the boys playing a home scene and the girls constructing with the blocks.

Taking the curriculum to the children may involve wrapping it up in the play the children are involved in, so that what they might consider 'work' indoors they will consider as play outdoors. Imaginative play indoors often involves reading and writing through, for example, note-taking in the doctor's surgery, adding up a bill in a shop, reading the newspaper at home. In schools involved in good outdoor play these activities are naturally added to imaginative play outdoors. And so children have notepads to take orders at a café, children write down the weather forecast for the farmer, children make maps of where the treasure is buried in a pirate scene. Children have opportunities to make number tags, labels for different events, scorecards for an imaginative sports scene. Staff organise number games in the gymnasium area where children have to stand at a particular number if wearing a particular colour, or games where children have to read what the card tells them to do – '4 skips' or '6 jumps', but alongside will be a drawing to help explain the words. Staff use chalk on the ground for all sorts of number and letter recognition games. They even use the playground surface as a piece of paper and have a game of rhyming where they use the surface of the playground to write down the words.

Simply by bringing aspects of the more formal curriculum outdoors may encourage some children to use that knowledge indoors, and make signs, notices, lists and the like, at the graphics table. As Paley (1984) found when she extended the play period, boys used the extra time to get involved in more work-orientated activities and the girls engaged in more imaginative play.

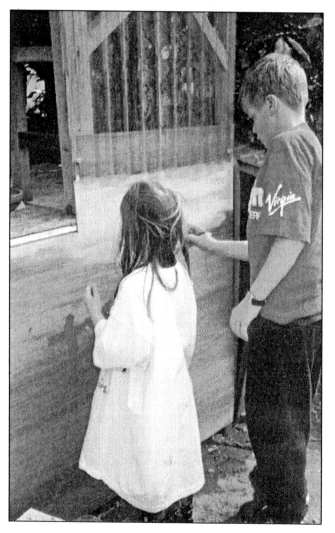

Figure 6.2 Year 6 child helping reception child paint the hide out.

In conclusion

All children have a right to access all activities and experiences in school. It would make sense that they do this in the easiest possible way. In this chapter it has been suggested that some children may prefer to play outdoors and that some children's play and behaviour may be different when outdoors compared to when indoors – they become more interested, more assertive, less inhibited or can concentrate more easily. This is so for both boys and girls but seems particularly pertinent to boys, who tend to want to play outdoors and who are more physically active, more keen to learn through exploration and interested in exploring superhero roles. It has also been suggested that some girls are not able to play as they would like or have the potential to do so outside, as boys tend to dominate many of the movable and constructive activities and staff are not present to support their endeavours.

In 1972 Hutt argued that boys and girls were different and needed to be treated as such: this would seem to be a message which needs revisiting. Girls seem more ready to fit the school system and as a consequence do well; on the other hand, many boys find school difficult and as a consequence are underachieving. To help all children reach their full potential it would seem beneficial to make the school system fit the needs of the children rather than expecting children to fit the school system. By offering the curriculum in an environment which children feel comfortable in and in a way they have knowledge of, may help boys to be more successful in learning. To enable girls to access the rich resources outdoors may involve staff supporting these children in their play and being with them to give them confidence. For this to happen staff need to make the outdoor play interesting, take the whole curriculum outdoors, and work and play alongside children in the outdoor setting. In this way all children, girls and boys, may have equality of access to the curriculum.

7: The role of the adult

The success of outdoor play rests with the staff. It is only when the whole staff support and enjoy outdoor play that it will work. A teacher recently said to me that she was not keen on imaginative play and so she did not have it! Sadly this can easily be the fate of outdoor play. When viewed as a peripheral activity which may or may not be provided, then outdoor play will only have a peripheral effect on children's learning. Where it is seen as a crucial part of education then it will be well provided for. As McMillan argues, the success of children's learning rests with the teacher. Lally (1991) argues that the role of the nursery teacher is a complex one; she sees it as a 'dynamic occupation' and one which requires continual investigation of themselves, the children and their families (p. xi).

The quality of the interaction between child and adult is central to higher-order functioning (Vygotsky 1978, Wells 1987). Higher order functioning is involved in play where children really have to think through ideas, analyse, and work with others to solve problems. This is about the development of intellectual self-control and leads to the development of thinking which is characteristic of logic, perseverance and concentrated thought. Play is not an easy game and requires a great deal from adults. For it to be successful adults need to interact, collaborate and, when necessary, facilitate and interpret. The interactionist approach highlighted by Bruce (1987) places a responsibility on adults to make sure children have a partnership role. Adults within the Foundation Stage, therefore, have roles to fulfil before, during and after children have been in the setting. Beforehand, staff need to think about the needs of the children in the setting and then plan accordingly. They need to think carefully about how materials, resources and equipment are to be set up.

While children are using the environment staff will be working with them. At the same time the staff will be assessing the effectiveness of the learning bays and observing the children at play. Afterwards, staff need to reflect on each day in preparation for the next day's experiences. The staff role is therefore the same as when working in the inside class, and involves bringing the children, the environment and the curriculum together. Continually referring to the guiding principles within this book and the principles for early years education within the Foundation Stage guidance (QCA 2000, pp. 11–12) will keep one's practice on the right track – with what to provide and how to provide it.

This chapter covers planning and evaluating learning, 'fine-tuning' as a session progresses, adult behaviour and female staff, joining in with children's play, skill teaching, the deployment of staff, setting up and starting points, tidying up, the role of parents, safety and analysing practice.

Planning for and evaluating learning

Quality planning, provision and evaluation do not come about through osmosis but from adults. Staff need to plan carefully, evaluate what has occurred in a day, observe what children are doing and saying, and evaluate the effectiveness of the resources. To ensure that the maximum is achieved from all learning bays, all will require adult involvement at some point and part of the planning is about where adults need to work. The planning needs to cover the provision of all the learning bays and whatever else that the staff may feel needs to be provided outdoors. It is not sufficient, therefore, to have a planning sheet for indoors with one small square devoted to the whole of outdoor play: the planning has to be as detailed as for indoors (see Figure 7.3). Once the two areas are viewed as one, then planning for both becomes much easier. Activities indoors can then support activities outside, and vice versa. But most importantly an activity can be placed in the position which will give the most to children, thereby making best use of all the available space. Whitehurst (2001) argues that practitioners need to plan activities and play and identify how adults can 'model, interact or play with children' when outside (p. 66) and that these features make for successful learning.

It is important to guard against listing the fixed structures in the outdoor area, such as the sandpit, climbing frame, house, boat, and then listing activities for each structure, as this means that curriculum planning is centred around a structure and not necessarily around learning. Staff who have fixed structures in their establishments tend to list learning areas and then decide how they can fit into the activity. So, for example, an imaginative play scene may be a pirate's ship, and it may be thought that the climbing frame will extend this play by being made into an island and so the materials and resources needed are set up on the climbing frame, plus the boat made by children the day before is made again; in this way the block area and climbing frame

Figure 7.1 Using the fixed structure for science work.

are part of one imaginative play scene: another time it might be part of the gymnasium. Otherwise, staff need to make sure they cross-reference to areas of learning, so that they check they are providing a balance across the physical areas. It may be that staff consider it important that children set up their own play and so, although the equipment will be provided, it will not be laid out, allowing children to do this from scratch. The fashion of setting up every area with some activity is a rather modern approach, but one which can be limiting. The planning, therefore, does not necessarily have to state what will be provided but could suggest possible questions to ask the children, or it may be suggested that adults should be deployed in that area from the beginning of the session. There should always be extra space on the planning sheet to include those activities that may not always be provided outdoors, but which need to be provided periodically. One such is painting; it may be felt that children's creative work seems somewhat stale and that, by providing a large sheet of paper attached to a wall, the children can paint in a different environment, with friends, on a large vertical surface. This may be the spark needed for some children to participate in more creative work and to give them fresh ideas.

Some schools use themes to support the planning and curriculum. This can have a narrowing effect, trying to fit absolutely every activity to a given subject and can waste valuable time. Themes should be there to support, not act as a straitjacket! The beauty of setting up the curriculum across the space – through learning bays or activity areas – is that one has already made sure that as a whole the activities are covering the curriculum/areas of learning. The activities themselves need to demonstrate a progression across time. For example in the planning sheet (Figure 7.4) the gymnasium area is about developing balance and the small motor about developing the skill of jumping. This will then be changed to another aspect of movement and motor control, but incorporating other curriculum areas where necessary. The horticultural or gardening bay has a theme all of its own and doesn't need any addition of a false one. This is called The Seasons. This learning bay is also a real experience and one that children can properly contribute to. It enables children to be involved in a worthwhile and authentic activity and enables them to really investigate something. Katz (1995) argues that children need real experiences and investigation is a natural way for children to learn; 'children are born natural scientists and social scientists' (p. 40).

Planning can only act as a guide: the ongoing assessment and the evaluation at the end of a day gives the more complete picture. Some staff record general observations as the session progresses, others spend time after the session in recording observations (see Figure 7.5). It is always important to note how the weather has affected play, either in a positive or negative way, and whether there are any problems with the two areas working together. One nursery, for example, found that the small blockplay area positioned outdoors was not being played with in a sustained fashion and children tended to flit in and out of the area. The reason for this could not be found, but staff moved the area to just inside the door and the behaviour became much more consistent.

Child study is central to our work, and more attention does need to be given to it and less to planning. The Whitehurst (2001) study argues that observing children at play needs to be bought into the adult role and that there is a need to 'observe and reflect' on what children are learning and how to further their learning (p. 72). In this class an adult is assigned to observe outside each day.

There are processes within play and outcomes of play; both need to be looked at to see the value of play. Wood and Attfield (1996), having looked at the relationship between play, learning and development, suggest there are critical questions to ask: 'What actually happens inside children's heads when they play? How do they become 'master players' and successful learners? What are children doing which is of value and interest to them in the immediate term, and may be of relevance in the longer term? (p. 125). These questions are expecting practitioners to analyse play generally and also analyse each child's play. This then leads to looking at the outcomes of play. Again Wood and Attfield suggest 'the outcomes can be enjoyment, peer group affiliation or status, rehearsal and repetition leading to mastery and control, or just fun and relaxation' (p. 125). They also argue that children do learn new things in their play. With regard to the fun and relaxation it is important to consider very carefully whether it is appropriate for an adult to be involved. But for the status of play to be raised it is important to identify both processes and outcomes.

Assessment of children is about observing them, writing down the information and finally making judgements. When making observations of children it needs to involve:

watching and listening to children while they are playing with other children, adults and alone,
talking to children about their play and work,
combining observations of children outside and in,
taking photographs of children playing,
discussing observations with parents and carers.

Given that some children, as has already been noted in the previous chapter, will behave quite differently inside and out, observations of them in both areas will give a more complete picture of their personality, their level of understanding and where they need help. A dated running record (see Figure 7.6) for each child is probably the simplest and most effective way of writing down observations and within this making comments about strengths, weaknesses, and what help is needed. Looking at the two examples given in Figure 7.6 it is quite staggering how much information has been gleaned about each child over a period of seven weeks. This type of written work is read by the staff and they use the records to help plan the curriculum.

By paying due regard to organisation and management we can update the environment to ensure that it works well. The evaluation will also need to reflect what needs to be set up again for the following day, or what can be left out as it is. Again, it is important to allow children to use equipment on a regular basis while making sure that they have enough equipment to change and modify their play.

'Fine-tuning'

Planning cannot be static and, as McLean (1991) demonstrates through the description of one teacher, there has to be constant 'fine-tuning' of the environment to fit the needs of the children's play. 'Fine-tuning' seems a particularly useful description for the minute-by-minute management of the space; it relies on the ability to scan the area and constantly watch the progress of play. It is about interacting with children, furthering the play situations, stimulating and feeding ideas to the children. Some children will need plenty of time to learn how to actually play and they will need adult support for this. Staff will need to spend time with children to make sure that play flows well.

Figure 7.2 Linking the principles for early years education and the guiding principles for outdoor play

Principles for early years education (QCA 2000)	Guiding principles for outdoor play
Effective education requires both a relevant curriculum and practitioners who understand and are able to implement the curriculum requirements.	10. Staff have to be supportive toward outdoor play.
Effective education requires practitioners who understand that children develop rapidly during the early years – physically, intellectually, emotionally and socially.	6. Outdoor play is central to young children's learning. And possibly more so to some children than others.
Practitioners should ensure that all children feel included, secure and valued.	9. Children need to be able to control, change and modify their environment.
Early years experience should build on what children already know and can do.	6. Outdoor play is central to young children's learning. And possibly more so to some children than others.
No child should be excluded or disadvantaged because of ethnicity, culture or religion, home language, family background, special educational needs, disability, gender or ability.	6. Outdoor play is central to young children's learning. And possibly more so to some children than others. 7. The outdoor classroom offers children the opportunity to utilise effective modes of learning – play, movement and sensory experience.
Parents and practitioners should work together in an atmosphere of mutual respect within which children can have security and confidence.	10. Staff have to be supportive toward outdoor play. 6. Outdoor play is central to young children's learning. And possibly more so to some children than others.
To be effective, an early years curriculum should be carefully structured. In that structure there should be three strands: provision for the different starting points from which children develop their learning, building on what they can already do;	1. Indoors and outdoors need to be viewed as one combined and integrated environment. 3. Outdoors is an equal player to indoors and should receive planning, management, evaluation, resourcing, staffing and adult interaction on a par with indoors.

Figure 7.2 *cont.,*

relevant and appropriate content that matches the different levels of young children's needs; planned and purposeful activity that provides opportunities for teaching and learning, both indoors and outdoors.	4. Outdoors is both a teaching and learning environment. 5. Outdoor design and layout needs careful consideration.
There should be opportunities for children to engage in activities planned by adults and also those that they plan or initiate themselves.	2. Indoors and outdoors need to be available to the children simultaneously. 8. Children need versatile equipment and environments. 9. Children need to be able to control, change and modify their environment.
Practitioners must be able to observe and respond appropriately to children.	3. Outdoors is an equal player to indoors and should receive planning, management, evaluation, resourcing, staffing and adult interaction on a par with indoors. 6. Outdoor play is central to young children's learning. And possibly more so to some children than others.
Well-planned, purposeful activity and appropriate intervention by practitioners will engage children in the learning process and help make them progress in their learning.	4. Outdoors is both a teaching and learning environment. 9. Children need to be able to control, change and modify their environment.
For children to have rich and stimulating experiences, the learning environment should be well-planned and well-organised.	1. Indoors and outdoors need to be viewed as one combined and integrated environment. 2. Indoors and outdoors need to be available to the children simultaneously. 4. Outdoors is both a teaching and learning environment. 9. Children need to be able to control, change and modify their environment.
Above all, effective learning and development for young children requires high quality care and education by practitioners.	all points

Figure 7.3 This weekly outdoor planning sheet demonstrates the link with the indoor curriculum and indoor play, offers starting points for play in each area, shows where staff will be supporting named children, what activities have been set up from the children's interest, how activities can be spread over a week, and what aspects of the activity staff may like to concentrate on. Obviously many other play situations will occur and staff will respond as the session progresses. There are 3 members of staff at this nursery and they decide on the day where each will start working and what their specific responsibilities will be.

Outdoor play	Monday	Tuesday	Wednesday	Thursday	Friday
w/b 1st June Notes	Connor and Megan's parents to bring in bits for imaginative play. Bring in mini-beasts from home!	Observe Jagdeep and Hardeep – physical skills	Potatoes		
Imaginative	Linked to indoors – moving house, available all week, changes made dependent on children's play . . .	Trucks, ropes, boxes, furniture, material, sticky labels, check-list of furniture for children to tick off . . .	Lunch boxes, thermos, extendable tape measures . . .	Staff input needed, particularly with children reading checklists and writing labels	
Construction	Filling in space – linked to moving house	No set-up. Saima and Em to make own construction with staff member	Filling in space. Using blocks, bricks – fitting into large wooden cubes, boxes, den	No set-up – Laura and Gina to make own building, staff support	Respond to children's ideas from the week
Gymnasium	Linked to story about bridges – moving around figure of 8 set-up without touching the ground	2 figures of 8 set-ups, one higher and one lower	Nests and ladders – strengthening arm muscles and tunnels, stretching horizontally	Combination of Monday and Wednesday arrangements	Arrangement to encourage use of prepositions – under, over, in, out, etc

Figure 7.3 *cont.,*

Small apparatus	Chalked letters, throwing ball onto named letter	Chalked letters using children's own initial letter	Writing letters on walls – to aim at	Bats and soft balls – batting practice for different levels – throwing ball to child and getting some to bat against wall	Open choice
Science	Following on from Jagdeep's and Junser's interest in mini-beasts' habitats – setting up dry, wet, covered and uncovered habitats to look at on Friday	Make books ready for recording information on Friday – special activity inside			Look at and record habitats
Gardening	Weeding, what constitutes a weed, gardening books	Weeding	M, R, J and E putting in potatoes	Billy, Ruth, Megan and Connor putting in potatoes	Planning sheet to decide what work needs doing next week

Other activities			Tape recorders and story and poetry tapes	Pastels and thick paper, big mats, canopy if sunny

Figure 7.4 Nursery class planning sheet – mid term, for 2 week period. This plan works very loosely from a theme as themes can take over, with time being spent trying to fit areas of learning into the theme which do not really fit. This plan concentrates on progression through the learning bay, for example the gymnasium has very specific movement intentions – be it balance, speed, endurance or attitudes such as perseverance. In this way by the end of a year children can be said to have experienced clear progression of learning. The plan reflects the seasons – for example the planting calendar and drawing of bluebells. This is but a fragment of what actually happens when plans are put into action. Clear links are shown between physical activity, language and mathematics. The learning bays together offer the whole curriculum with each bay emphasising some areas of learning more than others.

Food	Personal, social, emotional	Communication, language and literacy	Mathematics	Knowledge and understanding of the world	Creative	Physical
Imaginative – pizza delivery, shop inside or out	Cooperation, being approachable, working as a team, encourage girls to use bikes, encourage less forceful children	Lots of child-led conversations. Writing, and reading orders, maps, addresses, giving clear instructions	Money, writing numbers, totalling, spatial awareness, bike numbers, bike number plates	Locations, distances, routes, maps	Designing, making salt dough junk pizzas, garlic bread, designing and making logos and labels	Moving around area on bikes, writing skills, arranging food in boxes
Construction – setting up homes for delivery – simple and complex	Encourage 'having a go' approach, emphasis on safe building, encouraging reticent children, all children supporting this	Clear discussions, being able to visualise construction and describe	House numbers,	Science – sand tray, different size and weight of balls dropping from different heights to see impact re jumping	For some thinking about the aesthetics of the design, drawing out initial plan	Emphasis on lifting properly, not dragging. Using trucks to move things in. When using fiddly things – bands, pegs, etc – encourage children to do this themselves
Small motor – jumping	Helping each other improve movements, and discussing how to improve	Jumping onto associated words – jump, high, low, up, down, bounce, spring, pounce, kangaroo, hare, leap, wallaby, skip, gravity, hopscotch. Using the words as children move	Maths lang		Thinking through	Bending knees, jumping from one foot to other, skipping on own and with others, feet together and apart, hopscotch – older children

Figure 7.4 *cont.,*

Food	Personal, social, emotional	Communication, language and literacy	Mathematics	Knowledge and understanding of the world	Creative	Physical
Gymnasium – balance, chosen groups of children set up arrangements	Concentration, perseverance, giving time to achieve balance, not giving up, controlling environment, leadership					Concentrating on improving balancing techniques – not wobbling, hands aloft, looking ahead, posture
Gardening – put in carrot seeds, onion sets	Cooperation, thinking about what needs doing	Drill, depth, space, length, hole, furrow, dig, cover	Depth of holes, distances in planting	Weather, possible frosts, possible pests – carrot fly		Careful work, use trowels and spades with thought, piling up earth next to hole
Science, environmental – observational drawings – bluebells, purple spouting broccoli	Celebrate and appreciate different styles of drawing				Own work, celebrate diversity of styles, link to story writing about flowers and vegetables and flower/ veg fairies	
Quiet – books and tapes of stories and songs to do with food, making own jigsaws from postcards, writing stories about flowers and flower fairies	Confidence in getting to know songs and stories and so tell/ sing to others, give confidence to those less sure about own writing and creating skills, telling stories into tape recorder	Story procedure, rhyme, communicating ideas	Shape – rectangle, creating other shapes when making postcard, fitting together only one way possible	Food from around the world – postcards, usefulness of tape recorders		Scissor control
Other						

Figure 7.5 Assessment after planning from Figure 7.3

Imaginative	High quality play. PSE – cooperation, lengthy concentration span, groups 1–9 children, negotiation. Lang – copy writing, children reading own writing, emergent. Maths-lang – distance, time, size, space. Fun rearrangement of furniture. Planning – keep available alongside map work, KUW – link to technology inside. Lang – develop reading own writing, copy and emergent-offering written instructions in play, more numbered lists to complete.
Construction	Saima and Em more confident, went alone for 10 mins. PSE – good concentration. Maths – children surprised by quantity to fill large cube, realised needed to be systematic, if thrown in, packed in less. Was naturally extended to making 3-d filled in construction. Planning – Maths – go onto 2-d space, large horizontal surface area to fill, link to drawing (Creative, KUW)
Gymnasium	PSE – lot of unsure children, need adult input. Physical – effective strengthening of arm muscles. Planning – challenges to older children (Physical), stretching lang – stretch, pull, straight, taut.
Small apparatus	Very effective for boys, quality learning. Lang – very keen to be right, therefore concentration went up. Planning – lang-use words and phrases from imaginative work – how many, upright, forward, back, push, up, down, more. Physical – challenges to some children. PSE – involve particular girls.
Science	Final termers – Lang – worked well, they fed information back to all children during review time, very logical when explaining. PSE – Jagdeep and Junser argued re what they had found, but sorted differences through compromise. Lang – Josh and Josh wanted to be involved in recording. Good spoken lang – reasons given for wet and and covered – insects frightened (PSE), 'animals dry out', no water to drink (KUW).
Gardening	KUW and PSE – Nakita very interested – therapeutic. Maths – M, R, J, E – estimating depth and length. Planning – Maths – use rulers, children decided to leave forward planning, concluded (KUW) not much to do. Wait till Wednesday to check, they have put notice on board (Lang).
Other activities	Planning – not enough creative work. Move table outside for painting – possible stimulus – painting favourite houses, designing. KUW – painting large boxes, use wallpaper on wooden cubes for decorating. Lang – children to tell about their play scenes, adults to act as scribes. Jo, Esther, Ryan, Rachel, Josh to retell in review time. More written number work needed.

Figure 7.6 Example of running records

4.5	A lot of time playing solitary and watching what others were doing (sand). Does not talk a lot to other children. Talking to himself during imaginative play in house, pretending to peel an orange. Played with J in house pretending to be asleep. Loved playing with big bricks (with G and J), not a lot of talking though. Talked to me, pointed out correctly the colours of the bricks (R, Y, B, G) without being asked about it.
10.5	Needs language extension in English. Very immature syntax, usually only using nouns and verbs. Look at books with him 1:1. Drawing: did a very 'interesting' drawing of Mrs P. head separate from the eyes. Circle with bumps (photocopy)
11.5	Initiated several verbal exchanges with me. Needs a lot more basic vocab.
12.5	Same as above, played at the water tray for a long time, filling containers until they overflowed. Very pleased with it. Asked me to come and look.
13.5	Outside; very careful and attentive with C on the slide. Helped her up and also coaxed her down. Very gentle with her. 'Painted' the shed for a long time. Did not volunteer any observations verbally. Trying to talk to adults, but very limited vocabulary and syntax. Keeps nodding when adults talk to him, not sure how much he understands. Will talk to Mum and Dad.
14.5	Definitely does not understand 'again'. Finds it difficult to understand basic instructions. Should really be seen by a home language teacher to assess if his understanding in Urdu is any different.
24.5	Knows numbers up to 5, count and recognise.
7.6	Did milk today, knows who every label belongs to and who is in.
11.6	Cutting and gluing – problems with both. Needs lots more practice in this area.
15.6	Outside: clay work: stayed for a long time, making rolls for walls. Then proceeded to represent house in 2-d fashion, using rolls like pencil marks. Made a home with roof and 4 rooms. Then went on to put little bits of clay all on top of it. Said they were 'openings'.
17.6	Outside: ice balloons: very interested, stayed with the activity for a long time. Had to introduce word 'ice'. No concept of melting. Very surprised by it. Had difficulty with pronouncing words. Painted first picture of person with body, arms, legs, hair and 'willy'. Very pleased with himself. Emergent writing: used A to sign his name.
18.6	Drew self-portrait. Looked at himself and chose colours carefully.
21.6	Told milk label story today, volunteered to do it. Made a real effort to say sentences. He did extremely well, very pleased with himself. After milk told a whole long story to everybody – what he, his dad, and his sister had done in the park.

Figure 7.6 *cont.,*

In a period of 7 weeks not only had this child progress but also the staff had learnt a great deal about him and there is clear evidence of how the staff were supporting this child's development. The child in this period went from being quiet to being able to recount to the whole group an event in his life. He demonstrates clear empathy with other children, is willing to have a go at a range of activities and is learning from those experiences. His representational skills had developed so that he was able to actually draw himself and make a 3-d house. These are really significant developments over such a short period of time. However, much of what staff do in schools can be lost if it is not written down.

2. Boy, four-and-a-half-years old, 2nd term in nursery class

7.5   Played a lot with A in the hospital outside. He and A in leading roles, other children following. Needed to be reminded to look out for other children and not to run several times.
Spent quite a long time at the drawing table with I, both looking at the 'Goldilocks' book. He then did some drawing but not associated with the book.

10.5 Very willing to come and help with the brick house. Worked on the roof, overlapping tiles. Finished it all by himself. Remarked that it needed a chimney pot. When asked where, pointed out appropriate spot and stuck it on from behind. Was very pleased with the result. Very precise about his work with good, appropriate language: 'I need another layer'.

11.5 Spent quite a time with splatter painting outside. Really seems to enjoy art activities. Very concentrated play with big bricks outside. Was only one who really understood 'bond' and overlapping bricks. Very careful work. Then into imaginative play: 'This is Humpty Dumpty's wall'.
Electricity: had fine motor problems. Needed a lot of help with crocodile clips. Persevered though and understood principle.

11.6 Electricity: investigated further, again needed help because of fine motor problems. Cutting: does not hold scissors properly. Cuts upside down. Needs help and practice.

15.6 Spent quite a while at the clay table, rolling clay out flat, imprinting, making patterns. Commented on the 'cold' feel of clay.

17.6 Remembered really well what we had already said about Inuits, and Igloos. Was able to show on the globe where England and North Pole are. Knew that water freezes in the cold.

Again, this running record tells a great deal about this child and his learning. Although his overall development in the same period of time is not as obvious as the previous example, it does pick up on his personality and where he needs help. For example, he has good passive and active vocabulary and relocates information easily. It would be easy to let this child coast, however, he has fine motor difficulties, which need addressing and his interest in art to be seriously encouraged.

Fine-tuning is about adding resources which children may need or simply pointing children in the direction of resources which might fit their needs. It is about making sure one group of children's play does not encroach on another's, that some children do not dominate, and supporting children who are reticent. It is about making sure children all have enough choices, so that if two children move into role as painters and six other children want to join in, either more equipment is found for all of them, or some children are moved into another role. Fine-tuning is about pre-empting problems before they occur; it involves encouraging children to try out new skills and ideas, for example, the skill of climbing higher, or the skill of clearer negotiation. Children need to learn to think, to be confident in solving problems and to come to appreciate the useful effects of sharing, collaboration and negotiation. All these abilities need practice.

Fine-tuning also has to involve tidying up. The Gura (1992) research found that often blockplay was over by 10am because the area had been used and was basically used up and sometimes a mess. So staff need to discuss and agree at what point materials become too untidy. This will have to rely on the observation of the staff member at the time, and from the reaction of the children it will be possible to ascertain whether play has gone off-track and whether resources need to be sorted out. Staff also need to check whether constructions have been finished with and, if not, they should be left in situ or, if this is not possible, moved to a safe spot. Sometimes children wish to have their constructions displayed for everyone to see.

Fine-tuning is, therefore, a crucial part of our interaction with children. The ongoing assessment ensures we react to children's interests, difficulties and needs at the time and then help teach children or assist in their learning when appropriate.

Adult behaviour and female staff

The majority of early years staff are female but unfortunately outdoors is not a natural environment for many of them. They are, more often than not, keener to be involved in sedentary activities, which usually take place indoors. As a general rule, men tend to do the heavy, active, manual work, which usually takes place outdoors, and football and other sports activities are usually followed by men. This stereotype is reflected in the Foundation Stage setting, with many women preferring to work indoors at the creative activities and not wanting to venture into the outdoor play area.

Tizard *et al.* (1977) found that there were significant differences in the way staff worked indoors to outdoors. In nine centres where there were significant observations there was a trend for lower cognitive content in the staff behaviour outdoors, in seven cases the staff talked less to children in the garden, used more negative controls ('Don't do that') and in eight cases the amount of minimal supervision outdoors was greater compared with indoors. There can be more DIY-type jobs in the outdoor area which many women are not confident about (Gilkes 1987).

Paley (1984) acknowledges that she prefers the girls' play which tends to be quieter, more work-oriented, more 'let's-sit-round-mother-in-the-kitchen' type activity. She also admits that she appreciates the boys more when they are not playing boys' games or fantasy games but when they are being more like the girls! It is likely that many women working in the Foundation Stage may feel the same. However, as Paley further argues, it is important for staff to appreciate and understand boys' play, as males make up around half of the population.

'Teacher presence and modelling is an extremely powerful factor determining children's play activities' (Whyte 1983, p. 52). It is therefore not only important that staff use the outdoors effectively but also work with children to challenge sex stereotypes and thereby help to challenge these gender-conforming attitudes. Even more, their presence will raise the status of the activities. Children know which are the 'status activities' by the presence of the staff (Anning 1994). Children need to see female staff playing football, helping with pulling a truck full of children or playing with cars. Tizard *et al.* (1976a) found that preschool centres are markedly female-orientated, not only by virtue of the sex of the majority of the staff but also because of the amount of equipment that they have that is preferred by girls. The authors argue that the mismatch between the interests of boys and teachers starts early and that if staff want to reach out to boys then they need to interact more with boys and their interests, such as cars, garages, football and large construction. All children need to see female staff digging in the wild area, or see staff using the hammer. Girls and boys both need to see the female staff playing superhero roles. If staff do not get involved in boys' play then there are two adverse consequences. Firstly, boys will be denied adult input which all children need and benefit from, and secondly, boys' self-esteem will be effected as they will see that adults' interests are different from theirs. Adults getting involved in boys' play also means that aggressive behaviour is minimised.

In reading, children tend to follow behaviour along gender lines, with girls showing interest in their mothers' reading material and boys in fathers' reading material, which tend to be more action- and sport-orientated (Millard 1997). Reference books, magazines and comic strip are read more frequently by men and there has been a growth in magazines for men, such as GQ. Therefore, at school where most staff are women a concerted effort needs to be made to offer appropriate reading matter to boys and staff also need to show an interest in action and sport reading material. The skill required for reading non-fiction needs to be seen as being as valuable as reading a book from cover to cover. Within the outdoor area activities which support non-fiction reading, such as that in the horticultural or mini-beast area, need to be encouraged. Likewise, children need to see men sitting reading stories or helping with a piece of collage work. Such behaviour means that children, regardless of gender, will be accepted and supported and that any activity children decide to do now or in the future is supported. The differences between people have to be recognised; men and women *are* different, they do take on different roles, but no one is better than another by virtue of gender.

Not only have staff to acknowledge and deal with their own likes and dislikes, they also have to deal with societal attitudes. Many staff groups, having acknowledged the influences, are making superb use of the outdoor area. For example, making sure that outdoors and indoors are planned as one integral environment and so run simultaneously, means that outdoors becomes a more interesting place to be. Planning which covers the whole curriculum means that outdoors is not seen only as the physical exercise domain, but as a complete learning and teaching environment. The greater the amount of time children spend outdoors, the more staff plan and set up a variety of activities (Cullen 1993).

Where staff are using outdoors successfully, there are always seats about. This may also be one way of helping the more reticent adults to feel confident about working outdoors. When playing inside with children, staff tend to sit down or kneel next to a child, partly to rest the legs(!), but also so that they are at the child's level and eye contact is on the horizontal plane. Outdoors, where play involves much more movement, adults will have to converse from a standing position or while bending over, so if there are seats around the outdoor area, staff can make sure they and the children can stop to have more intimate conversations.

Work outdoors is often heavier than indoors, involving moving furniture and equipment about. Chapter 4 includes many ways to help alleviate this. Where there are jobs to be done which include carpentry skills and building and staff do not feel confident, the answer may be to call in help from parents or governors or any other volunteers, paying due regard to health and safety issues. Once outdoors is an interesting environment, and staff see how to work within the environment, then hidden talents will blossom forth from the staff!

Joining in with children's play

Being part of children's play is probably the most difficult job we have to do, because to get it right requires a lot of effort. The adult involved has to be thinking all the time about how to help the play and learning along. But it is essential to be part of children's play otherwise 'children left alone to play do not develop imaginatively; after a time much of their play becomes repetitive and lacking in progression . . . Without the help of a teacher setting the environment and providing the suggestions, children reach stalemate and their play becomes intellectually aimless' (Manning and Sharp 1977, p. 15). Although staff have a watching brief over all activities, it is clear that in some schools staff get more involved in some activities than others and it tends to be those activities which are more sedentary.

Cullen (1993) found that the quality of play in the outdoor sandpit area was very low level in terms of physical, creative, social and cognitive dimensions. She argues that adults need to intervene by questioning, adding resources and joining in the play. The Hutt *et al.* (1989) study found that at the collage table, where an adult was in almost permanent attendance, the play was high quality and included wide-ranging conversations, but at the sand and water area there was no adult present and the play was low quality and repetitive. Kostelnik *et al.* (1986) suggest that quality collaborative play can occur with the intervention of an observant teacher. They also suggest how adults can enhance superhero play into complex socio-dramatic play episodes and still involve physical activity. Intervention therefore can stop the rather meaningless superhero play that sometimes occurs. Blatchford's (1989) study of children during the primary playtime similarly suggests that adult involvement in the play could improve the play quite considerably.

The impact on behaviour when teachers are not involved in play is even more apparent where boys are involved. Davies (1991), looking into children's adjustment to nursery class, found that boys' adjustment to nursery was not as successful as girls'. She argues that as staff are not visiting those areas where boys tend to play, then there is little chance of developing their positive learning attitudes. If staff spend more time inside with the creative or quiet activities, then it will be the girls who benefit from the interaction and not the boys. Given the growing concern about boys' adjustment and subsequent success in school, it is clear that staff do need to ensure that all areas within the class and outdoor space get equality of input from the staff. Davies suggests that staff should check whether the time planned actually matches the time spent on various activities, in order to ensure the equality of adult participation and intervention in all areas of the setting.

Sometimes it is appropriate to become involved in children's play to defuse confrontational situations which children cannot sort out themselves. Without this support the play can disintegrate or end in unresolved standoffs. In role, children can either be led into a sidetrack of the play or into a new play situation, if staying in the present one may cause arguments over the direction of play, the use of resources, or over who is playing which role. In the McLean (1991) study, Nan, one of the teachers observed, was very keen to create a good environment for the children to play in. She made sure they had a lot of space and resources to work with, but she was also involved in attracting 'particular children to specific areas, to aid in the formation of the desired peer groups, to extend children's play and avoid potential peer conflicts' (p. 101). Most of her strategies were very subtle, so children were unaware of her role.

Some staff are reticent about joining in with children's play, arguing that they are concerned that children will be interrupted and that their play is a private affair. This is a valid point and children, whatever they are doing, should be credited with some degree of privacy. Paley (1986), talking about joining in with children's play, says, 'often I drift around the edge of their knowing without finding a place to land' (p. 131). However, this concern does somewhat contradict how children can behave. One of the wonderful, yet quite difficult, traits of young children is their ability to tell you when to go away. They will walk away when they have had enough of you, they will say 'Bye' in the middle of your talk; they will say 'No thanks' when you offer them what you think is the most stimulating activity going. So children will say, in the right environment, whether they want you or not. Sometimes it is appropriate to say, 'Can I join you?' At other times it may be appropriate to get into role as you approach. It is important to assess *why* you are joining in and how this will help the children involved. Where children have control of their play by virtue of time, space, resources, supportive staff, and an ethos which encourages children's independence and control, they will feel confident to involve adults when they want to. There will always be difficult situations, as Nan found, and when she did not become heavy-handed, issues were resolved (McLean 1991).

Staff also need to be involved in children's play to offer support. This is a crucial component of children's play and one which ensures the continuation of quality play. Dunn and Morgan (1987), looking into play patterns in nursery and infant classes, found that children's play at school was actually helping to reinforce stereotyped role models and behaviours. Studies, such as those of Halliday *et al.* (1985), show that stereotypical play choice is reduced when staff get involved in children's play. Actually being part of children's play, and thereby challenging prejudice as it arises, has to be part of the whole package of prejudice-removal from the Foundation Stage, in effecting a change in children's attitudes. But equally, children need to work through stereotypical ideas through their play (Bruce 1987).

How prejudice is challenged has to be considered. Becoming the heavy-handed adult may have little effect, but challenging prejudice when in role as part of imaginative play may have more impact. Sometimes classes use drama to show what sort of behaviour is and is not acceptable and report that this has a lasting effect on the children.

Morgan and Dunn (1990) found that some resources had 'high status' and these gave rise to disputes about access, to unwillingness to share and, in almost all cases, the winners in the disputes were the boys. A classic example of this is bikes. Bikes seem to inherit a status level all of their own! No one says that 'bikes are best', no one says 'the red bike is the best of all', but this is what happens. What then follows is that some children, mostly boys, will race to get the bikes, to get the 'best' bike. These children will do just about anything to achieve their aim, and this may include harming other children and damaging equipment. They will then do anything to stay on the bike for as long as possible. The reasoning behind this behaviour is that a perceived high status toy gives high status to the owner, therefore the child's self-esteem goes up. When the child has to give up the bike their self-esteem goes down, and they feel unimportant and often lost – their only direction is to seek out the high status toy again. In classes where staff plan and get involved with children's play this does not happen and children show much less interest in bikes as a means to raise their self-esteem. In case study 4 (see Chapter 2) children were able to choose what toys they would like to play with every Friday. At the beginning of the term, some children would always choose bikes, but by the end of the term bikes were rarely chosen for a free choice activity, as there was so much else going on. Incidentally, I do wonder if some staff who simply put lots of bikes out and little else and then spend their time controlling who is on or off the bikes, are playing out some power game of their own. Unless we are part of children's play how can we help to challenge stereotypical play and stop such gender disputes and also make sure that all activities are seen as worthwhile and none are seen as less important than others?

Davies and Brember (1994) found that boys were perceived to be less well-adjusted to nursery school and Davies (1991) found in the nursery settings that boys were seen by the teachers as being much more aggressive, uncooperative and with more learning difficulties than girls. This may be a perception rather than a reality and goes back to Paley's comment that she found it more difficult to cope with the more active play of the boys. Davies argues that certain areas within the nursery may need to be timetabled so that all children can have equal access and a fair experience of all resources. In this way children would not always be choosing the same equipment and thereby reinforcing unhealthy behaviour patterns. It might also mean that the boys would become calmer and the girls' activity level would be raised.

Morgan and Dunn (1990) found that the 'invisible' children in the class tended to be girls and the 'visible', and those demanding most teacher attention, were the boys. Again, unless adults interact with children and have observation at the heart of their work, they will be unlikely to pick out those children who are fading into the background and those who are taking over.

It may be that a child needs support because they are unsure in the situation of play outdoors or within one particular learning bay. With an adult there, a child can enter a play situation without feeling threatened and can find out about the potential of an activity with the help of an adult. An example from a play situation may help to demonstrate the importance of adult presence.

Two boys confident when working outside, had illicited the help of the teacher in building a house, using crates, planks and boxes. Emily entered the scene saying she wanted to make a house. The teacher did not want to disturb the play situation of the boys by taking some of the crates, so suggested that Emily and she build a house using barrels, ladders and large plastic cubes, which they did. Emily continued to watch the boys. Two other girls joined Emily.

The next day, Emily approached the teacher and asked if they could make a house using crates. The teacher and Emily filled a truck with crates and set off to build a house. Manmit,

Gurjit and Timothy (the boys who had built the house the day before), came over and wanted to build the house, and they immediately assumed positions of control. The teacher said no, and suggested another play situation for them. Emily described what she was doing – 'building a back door, a front door, two seats'. Timothy had wandered back by this time and had arranged two barrels at the side of Emily's house. He said, 'This is the back door.' Emily disagreed but then said, 'Alright, let's have two doors.' Two other girls entered the scene and helped Emily. When they had finished, the three sat down and Emily, with much pleasure said, 'Look at this building we have done.' Timothy continued to stay on the side lines. The teacher was called away but Emily's game continued. She stayed in charge and Timothy stayed on the periphery. (Bilton 1989, p. 63)

The teacher's role in this situation seems crucial and makes the job of fine-tuning very apparent. She made herself available to the children and was someone they could play with. She played with Emily and protected her from children wishing to dominate the scene, steered other children away to a new scene, and she steered Emily on the first day to construct a new building, so making sure the boys' play was not disturbed, she stayed quiet when Timothy had made a door and allowed Emily to deal with the situation. Given time and adult input, Emily should be able to discover the joys of a new resource, play with boys and gain in confidence through being in charge.

However, the length of time an adult needs to stay to encourage a reticent child to work without adult support will vary. The results from the Halliday *et al.* (1985) study into influencing children's choice of activities at kindergarten through teacher participation, found that girls stayed at the blockplay while the adult was there but moved away once the adult left. The authors argue that teachers *do* influence play choice by their presence and involvement, but they also need to stay long enough, and on enough occasions, for children to discover or come into contact with enough satisfying aspects of the play, so that they will wish to return to it with a friend or alone.

Skill teaching

Rather than merely participating in outdoor activities children need to be taught specific skills, just as children need to be taught specific skills with regard to, say, reading. Skills are generally taught in a PE or Movement lesson but often, when staff move outdoors, they do not see it as their duty to teach motor skills. Practice, encouragement and instruction are crucial for the development of mature patterns of movement (Gallahue 1989).

In a study by Miller (1978) it was found that three- to five-year-olds when given a structured movement programme, improved their fundamental movement patterns beyond those children who had not been given a programme and had been left to themselves. Wetton (1983) was concerned as to why four-year-olds used a climbing frame less than the three-year-olds. She concluded that the four-year-olds had been given no help or challenge in developing their skills beyond what they could find out themselves: the adults had not been helping the children to gain new skills.

Cullen (1993) argues that preschool children will not achieve physical objectives or gain skills if they only have a free play programme. But she also issues a warning about the planned supervised obstacle course, which, although it addressed the need for skill improvement, created problems as children spent a great deal of time waiting for their turn. Wetton (1998) highlights the centrality of observation and assessment in a structured play environment. She argues that sometimes children can become 'wanderers' even in a well set up environment; these are the children who are unable to access this type of free choice environment. There are also the children who do not have suitable clothing or footwear, who lack the necessary negotiation skills or have immature motor development, who will also be excluded from many of the activities. This demonstrates the need to actually observe, assess and then teach children the necessary skills, to be instrumental in supporting them in their efforts and making sure practical matters such as clothing do not stop them having equality of access. A balance, therefore, needs to be achieved between free choice and intervention (Boorman 1988). Direct teaching is best for teaching the best way to move, refining and combining skills, and indirect teaching encourages exploration, discovery and combining of movements (Gallahue 1989).

Cullen (1993) suggests that staff tend to be vague about physical development and talk in general rather than in specific terms. Staff need to be skilled in the systematic evaluation of motor skills in order to help children develop. Not only should the skills and activities be part of the planning, but staff need to note down what skills they are hoping specific children should be learning next. Some children, for example, may not know they that need to bring their hands into their body when catching a ball, some children may be ready to throw high and accurately, to throw to someone else; most children need to be shown that a ball will go further if kicked from a run rather than from standing still. Likewise, with movement on the apparatus, children need ideas on how to move around, for example, stepping up a ladder, balancing without holding on or hanging and moving under monkey bars. Wetton (1988) offers a useful source of games to be played with nursery and infant children.

But equally, children need to learn the skills of getting on with others, of being able to negotiate with someone so that both parties feel they have succeeded. Through imaginative play and construction where children are working toward a common goal, children need to refine their skills of collaboration. Staff need to point out to children the consequences of their actions and if they continue, say, to argue, the tower, tunnel or whatever, will not get built. Children can be given pointers as to how to cooperate, such as talking about what they all anticipate the final product might look like, or actually stopping an imaginative scene, moving children out of role to discuss what has happened so far in the play and where children want it to go next. The children can then go back into the play scene and hopefully carry on with more success. Sometimes they need to be left to sort out difficulties themselves, thereby consolidating learning and developing their understanding.

Costello (2000) argues that there is a direct relationship between thinking and behaving and thinking well and behaving well. An educated adult is one with knowledge and skills in a number of areas but is also one who thinks critically and carefully about beliefs, attitudes and values and acts in morally appropriate ways (p. 102). Part of our role is to help children think. The debate about thinking skills has been raised again with the introduction of citizenship education in schools. But to understand citizenship one has to be able to think for oneself first. Helping children to think critically means not teaching a body of knowledge but providing an environment, in which children are able to debate issues, evaluate arguments, question evidence, formulate theories. Stories and videos can be one way to open up debates, but, equally, as we work and play alongside children, our questioning of how and why things happen and are done in a particular way will raise children's desire to question. Margy Whalley (1998) describes how one local teacher calls the children from her nursery as having 'the Pen Green Syndrome' (p. 171) – it strikes me these children have simply been taught to think!

Deployment of staff

When indoors and outdoors are available simultaneously, it is preferable to have one member of staff indoors and one outdoors. Any more adults can then be assigned to areas as agreed by the staff group. The rota will be flexible so that staff can react to the children's needs and although initially assigned to one particular area, can then move between play scenes both indoors and outdoors as needs arise. In some situations where the play is so intricately wound up with a particular member of staff it may be necessary for that member to go indoors if the group of children want to and have a member of staff from indoors swap with them. Where there are only two adults available, one indoors and one outdoors, this swapping can still occur. It may be that children move indoors and outdoors a lot, for example, when using the writing equipment to make signs or constructing something from reclaimed material to use in the play situation outdoors, and they can move between the two areas on their own. It may be in some circumstances that staff can have a quick conversation and pass on any relevant information about the play and how the adult has been involved.

If there is only one member of staff for two areas, such as an infant class, then it is important to discuss procedures with the head teacher and to seek extra help. Some infant and primary schools have outdoor play for the under-fives for the entire day, some make it available for part of the day, some organise outdoor activities for groups of children, some group classes together and split the staff between indoors and outdoors and some timetable the first part of the day for play in both areas. Whitehurst (2001), looking into her own practice with reception children, concluded that the inner courtyard just outside the classroom could be utilised by the children and without adult presence all the time. In fact this would help further promote children's independence (p. 62).

The Cleave and Brown (1991) study highlights one school which joined three classes of children together for the afternoon and then used one of the classrooms and the adjacent outdoor area for children to simultaneously use indoors and outdoors. Two teachers stayed outdoors and one indoors and, when an extra adult was available, children were able to use the wheeled toys on the school's playground. It is still important for staff to play with children in the outdoor setting and the research concerning staff involvement and participation in children's play is as relevant in the infant setting as the nursery setting.

In many infant settings teaching assistants/learning support assistants are being employed to support the Foundation Stage teacher. Whether it is a teaching assistant or trained NNEB, all members of staff can work outside as long as agreement has been reached with the head teacher. If inside and out are viewed as one teaching and learning environment, made up of two halves, then it would seem to follow that all staff can work in all areas. What cannot be acceptable, is where the TA is relegated to outside with the teacher constantly working inside.

Setting up and starting points

If outdoors has equal importance to indoors then the right amount of time has to be given to setting it up. Probably 20 minutes to a maximum of 45 minutes is ample time to allow for this, but how long it takes is dependent on what is being set out and how far equipment has to be moved. Once the resources are easily stored, for example in a trolley or in labelled boxes, the amount of time it takes to move things will lessen. Obviously this setting up needs to take place before the children arrive, otherwise fewer staff are available for the children to play with. If it is left until the start of the session then parents do not get as much opportunity to talk to the staff. It also sends a message to the children, parents and staff that outdoor play is not very important.

Setting up is about giving children ideas, posing questions, teaching a specific skill, offering ideas by laying out books alongside resources. Photographs of children in imaginative play scenes, easily taken at the nursery, can act as an ideas bank for children. The mere presence of an adult alongside some resources may start a scene off. Sometimes children will use these ideas, or they may ignore them and start with their own. As long as children are secure in the knowledge that they have control over their environment then quality learning will occur.

One way of helping children to get started in a play scene or to develop their play is through storying, and this is also a means by which adults can get involved in children's play. Children will use stories from television in their imaginative play, partly because these are stories that they know. Staff can add to a child's repertoire by telling stories beforehand and gathering the necessary resources for the story to be acted out. An obvious example is *Goldilocks and the Three Bears*. However, whatever the story, it has to be well resourced. I have seen a set up of three bowls, three stools and three beds and nothing else, with the expectation that children will have quality play and then staff are surprised when the children do not play for a long time and have very low level conversation. Many stories can be used; for example, in one school a teacher based the whole curriculum around the story of *Watership Down* and activities in the nursery incorporated themes from the story (Meadows and Cashdan 1988). Stories such as *The Enormous Crocodile, The Town Mouse and the Country Mouse, The Animals of Farthing Wood, The Enormous Turnip* are possibilities; some stories would obviously be told over a period of time. The Suzanne Gretz stories are quite detailed and complicated and yet the stories are actually reasonably short. These stories have lots of potential for acting out a variety of themes. Some children would relish the stimulus, others would not want to follow such a theme. Some children, who have little experience of play and need help in how to play, would find such a stimulus very helpful.

The involvement of staff would of course be based on the children's needs. This approach may also benefit some children who are not used to the forms and meanings of narrative, the acting out of the story would mean they could use the familiar vehicle of conversation to interpret the story. This would reflect the approach of the teacher in the Dombey (1993) study who was able to introduce children to the narrative processes by using the familiar conversational approach during storytime.

Tidying up

Children can be involved in the tidying up process. This would begin outside and eventually move inside. Children who are taught how to do so can carry planks, stack crates, blocks and bricks, arrange equipment in labelled trolleys, fold material and the like. They need to be taught the correct methods and they need to be given time to become proficient. Older children will support and help the younger ones once the system is established. It is wasteful of staff and children's time to tidy up for them. Through tidying up children learn to respect each other and their school environment, to cooperate, to be responsible ('now this needs tidying up'), to match shapes and sizes, to problem solve, to read signs and labels, to think ahead ('if I do this, this will happen, therefore I'd better stop'). It initially takes more effort from the staff to get tidying up running well, but once in place it is far easier and more useful than doing it for the children.

   Children can also be involved in the daily and seasonal clearing. For example, children enjoy and learn from sweeping up leaves. The actual skill of wielding a brush is difficult – one has to learn to be aware of both the brush end and the pole end so one doesn't knock anyone. Arm muscles are strengthened through the motion of sweeping. Children will need to work together and cooperate to get the leaves into piles, into bags, onto the compost heap. Finally children are filled with a sense of pride at their achievement. I was amazed recently to see a parent sweeping and weeding in a nursery class garden – what a waste for the children. Social and emotional development can be fostered through clearing up, putting out, general cleaning and sweeping, weeding, sorting and throwing out. In this way children get a sense of ownership and so pride and they are then keen to look after the environment. In case study 2 (Chapter 2), children saw an old bucket in the rubbish and suggested it could be used as a planter in their outdoor area. This was because they clearly cared about their environment.

Role of parents

What is the role of the parent and carer in outdoor play? Parents need to see the purpose and benefit of what is done in the Foundation Stage. This is very pertinent to outdoor play, as it is quite alien to many people. Staff want parents and carers to support what they are doing, so it is their responsibility to convey its relevance. Margaret McMillan felt that if parents could watch their children at play and staff could interpret the play, then parents would be able to see the reasons for it. Talking to parents about the work in the setting, having regular parent meetings focusing on aspects of the work, encouraging parents to come in, or better still, having somewhere that parents could watch and not be seen, and so on, are all helpful in enabling parents to see the relevance of early years education. A school in Hartlepool asked a group of parents to be the leading participants in a project to make a video of the nursery in action. One of the difficulties with such activities as parenting classes is that they can appear to be patronising. However, this project, by asking the parents to actually do the work of making the video, did not patronise anyone and parents' self-esteem and understanding of the preschool curriculum were increased and they felt more involved with the education of their children. Parents clearly took ownership of their own children's education as a result of their participation in the project (Robson and Hunt 1999). This seems a very worthwhile approach to the involvement of parents and was successful because the staff trusted the parents to be able to do what was asked.

   However, even more important is the contact between staff and parent to support that parent's child. This is when parent and teacher can convey information and tackle any difficulties together. A part of this partnership is conveying to every parent, on a regular basis, the achievements of their child. Bartholomew (1996) talks about parents being 'partners in observation', and that this sharing between parents and teachers plays a central role in supporting children in their learning (p. 54). Talking to a parent about something the child has done, which they have enjoyed and learned from, will not only help to raise the self-esteem of parent and child, but also convey more vividly the work of the Foundation Stage and the reasons for working in a particular way. This can be done by systematically ensuring each parent is spoken to within, say, a one or two week period.

Staff find some parents easier to talk to than others, some parents make themselves more available and are more confident than others. Just as there are children who take up more of the staff's time and there are children who fade into the background, so too are there such parents. But all have a right to celebrate their child. A comment could be along the lines of: 'Darren did a superb picture today, did you see it?', which can then be followed by a comment about why it was good, and a discusson of the level of concentration, the detail in the picture, the deliberation over colour mixing and matching. And it can be a comment on children playing outside: 'Erin worked really hard outside today, when she was playing at being a post lady'. This could involve a discussion about an interaction between two children and how they cooperated, how they sorted out difficulties together and how long they concentrated. In this way the parent is finding out that through play children learn to cooperate and negotiate, and that through play children are demonstrating that they can concentrate and that outdoor play has a purpose to learning and understanding. It does not have to be put into 'education-speak', but does need to be positive. Comments about children at play celebrate the child and the methods by which they learn.

Photographs of children at work and play can support discussions with parents and can be the focus of a discussion. They can be displayed with written information and transcripts of what the children were saying for parents and carers to view at their leisure. This is the approach adopted by the Emilio Reggio schools in Italy. A school is Berkshire continually takes photographs of children and staff at work as a record for parents, to support displays, but also to go onto the school web site, for children to access to use in their work, concerning what they will be doing, what they have done and so on. As they say, a picture can paint a thousand words! Books can support verbal discussions and photographic evidence. A shelf with books and magazines for carers to borrow, is a useful addition to any Foundation Stage class. In terms of play an accessible book for carers could be something like Christine Macintyre's *Enhancing learning through play* (2001).

Safety

Staff have to consider the issue of safety, whether the environment is indoors or outdoors. It has to be considered particularly closely outdoors as children are more active and will be moving around on equipment, which they do not tend to do indoors, except where there is an indoor climbing frame or wooden cubes. In recent times, safety in the outdoor area has centred around the need to have safety surfaces. However, safety in school is about much more than this. It is about making sure that equipment and resources are not dangerous and that staff and children do not behave dangerously. This is an ongoing and daily responsibility. Many safety issues are tied up with common sense. However, it is worth looking at evidence as to what causes accidents. Avery and Jackson (1993) found that the majority of accidents occurred when differing age groups were together, when children attempted something beyond their capabilities and when the equipment had been poorly maintained. The most common accidents were on swings, slides and climbing frames. Tina Bruce (1987) argues that having equipment out infrequently can cause accidents. For example, if the climbing frame comes out say once a week, children can be so desperate to use it that they may do things they would not normally, such as pushing others, getting on too quickly, not thinking before they make a move and then accidents happen.

Staff need to check on a daily basis that equipment is safe, free from splinters and that nothing is broken. Metal equipment needs to be wiped after rain because it can be slippery when wet, equipment can get dangerously hot, so needs covering up until the children use it. When setting up the equipment staff need to check it has been put together properly and is secure. When assessing the safety of equipment it is important to get down at the child's level, to see if it is safe at their height and that there are no dangerous bits, particularly at their head level. As staff work and play with children it is most important to keep a careful eye on safety and check that children are behaving safely. In this way staff can anticipate problems and avert them. They need to keep an eye on those children whom they know probably have not yet reached an appropriate level of understanding of the potential dangers of the situations that are provided for them, and on those who are simply not used to the equipment or the level of freedom given in the Foundation Stage setting.

Teaching children to use equipment safely will greatly help in reducing accidents (Avery and Jackson 1993), and is another aspect of the common-sense strategy to ensuring safety. Children need to be safety conscious and they can be asked about issues to do with safety in their class and be part of the discussion process. When they are using equipment children need to know that they should only do what they feel safe doing. The moment a child feels unsure is when they will wobble, fall and hurt themselves. So although staff will set challenges and children will set challenges for themselves, they need to be told to go only as far as they feel safe. And children will be able to know when they have reached that point.

The accident study found that, where children were of different ages, accidents were more likely to occur. Children, therefore, need to know that just because someone else can do something does not mean they have to have a go. More confident children must be aware of children who are less confident, so guidelines about no pushing or pulling on any apparatus, especially climbing apparatus, will have to be made clear to all the children. They also need to be told that vehicles cannot be put under climbing frames, they cannot climb with heeled or loose footwear, and they cannot climb in long clothing. If there are parts of the garden where it is not possible to see round a corner, children need to know to take it wide, or staff may need to put up a barrier so that children have to go round wide of the corner.

Many schools have rubber tyres which are quite heavy and they have found that they are dangerous if rolled. These should be used only for sitting on or for arranging for building purposes. A hoop can be used for rolling purposes instead. Milk crates are very useful for loading into trucks, making into buildings and constructions, for blocking in an area. They are not safe for climbing on, but if a piece of wood is attached to the underneath surfaces and then turned over they can be made into level stepping stones.

Parents will also need to be involved in making sure children come in footwear and clothing which enables them to move easily. Where staff are able to demonstrate the benefits of their work, parents are more able to see the reasons for requests such as sending children in shoes which they can climb, jump and run in. A box of spare shoes is always handy in case children do not have safe footwear.

Schools do need to make an assessment of the safety of their establishment, both indoors and outdoors. This is known as a risk assessment and focuses on the safety of materials. This can include not only whether a piece of equipment is safe, but also whether its positioning is safe. Equipment put close to a doorway can create a real safety hazard, equally a cluttered space or area lacking in space can be a safety problem. So when making a risk assessment everything has to be looked at: resources, equipment, amount of space, positioning and use of equipment. A safety document written by the staff group makes safety issues clear to other visiting staff and parents and can be reassessed and updated periodically. The safety representative and the P.E. adviser from your local authority will of course be able to give advice.

Esbensen (1987) argues that when purchasing outdoor equipment staff should have a good knowledge of child development and anthropometrical data, so only equipment which is right for the age group and height of the age group is bought. It needs to be robust and strong enough to withstand use by many children and withstand the effects of the weather. Wood is the preferred material, then wood and metal and then metal on its own. Most quality wooden material is expensive, such as that made by Community Playthings, but it will last (see Appendix). So in the long run, it will be more cost effective to buy the more expensive, well-made products.

The worst injury a child can sustain is that of falling from a height and hitting their head. Shock-absorbent surfaces can be put in to make sure that if a child does fall they will not be permanently injured. However, it needs to be clear that a safety surface will not keep anyone completely safe and children can still get broken arms and the like. And there is evidence that safety surfaces can give a false sense of security to both children and adults. The important consideration is what is called the critical fall height. The maximum safety surface will take a critical fall height of 2.5 metres, in other words, if a child falls from this height onto the maximum safety surface, they will not sustain a permanent head injury. The European standards which dictate the need for a safety surface with climbing apparatus only applies to fixed equipment. Movable equipment such as A-frames, planks, ladders, crates, etc., do not need safety surfaces. This type of equipment can be placed on mats or on the grass. As already stated elsewhere in this book, Foundation Stage outdoor play is not about fixed climbing frames and is the last piece of equipment I would buy. Monkey bars, or ropes attached to posts and some kind of tree house would be my only suggestions for fixed equipment. The skills of climbing, swinging, balance and coordination can more easily be acquired on movable equipment.

Although safety is very much a case of common sense, staff groups have to be aware of liability and need to make a thorough risk assessment so that they can categorically say that safety issues have been addressed. Most important is the attitude of the staff. The manic, let off steam behaviour that one can see in some early years settings is caused by children not having enough to do, who are bored and have not had their play channelled or their ideas engaged. In this atmosphere accidents are many. A well resourced, well managed and cared for environment, with children and staff working together will have very few accidents. As the day progresses staff do need to keep a watchful eye, observing, scanning, anticipating problems, knowing who may need what help, but at the same time giving children a degree of privacy. Finally, we need to appreciate that children need challenges to help them become self-regulatory in their safety. RoSPA argues that children need challenges: 'It is essential to their healthy growth and development. Children need to learn about risk, about their own capabilities and to develop the mechanism for judging it in controlled settings' (Cook and Heseltine 1999, p. 4). Children do not need to be faced with hazard and danger, but they do need to experience risk and challenge. There are challenges in all aspects of life – whether it be the challenge and potential risk of reading a new word or of climbing up a plank.

Analysis of practice

Sometimes it is helpful to look systematically at your practice to check whether what you think is happening is the true state of affairs. Davies (1991) argues, for example, (in connection with which areas of the class are used and which are not), that 'time planned' does not always match up to 'time spent'. In the course of a week it would be quite simple for each member of staff to take a notebook and jot down which areas they work in and for how long. In this way it will be quite apparent whether some areas of the classroom and outdoor space are getting a lot of adult intervention and whether others are getting little. The situation can easily be rectified, the observation schedule in the study by Dunne and Bennett (1990) clarifies what demands, and the number of demands, that are being made on a teacher. This type of schedule could be used in the outdoor setting to look at whether best use is being made of staff time.

A similar grid could be devised for analysing outdoor play, looking at interaction between children and children, and staff and children. The interactions of interest could include demands for staff to get involved in play, demands to sort out disputes over resources, demands to find a resource, demands of a routine nature (those concerning going to the toilet or getting a coat) (see Figure 7.7). These demands could be noted down in a 20-minute period. It may be that, for example, many of the demands concern disputes over bikes and that these take up a lot of staff time. It will then be necessary to analyse why this is happening. Staff will need to look at the organisation and management issues raised in Chapter 1, and consider the number of resources, whether there is a culture of high- and low-status toys or whether the children are not able to negotiate. Staff may want to go further and analyse who is making particular demands; it may be that the demands are about children wanting staff to play with them. It may be worth checking to see if only certain children are asking for this and others are not getting as much adult input. There may be organisational problems, or it may be something more subtle, involving the expectations within the class and that children are not expected to be autonomous and think through their own ideas and so they then simply access equipment which does not involve much input from them. By making changes to what is available in the outdoor area, by working more closely with groups of children, these demands could be lessened and in this way staff can use their valuable time better.

Another method of recording that could be used is the Effective Early Learning's three types of 'engagement' to analyse your practice with children. This describes:

Figure 7.7

Type of demand	Number of demands in 20 minutes
Play	
Disagreements	
Find resource	
Fix something	
Routine – eg. toilet	
Talk	

    sensitivity to children;
    stimulation of children;
    giving some autonomy to children about what they want to learn;
as three types of interaction an adult may have with a child (Pascal *et al.* 1997).

They found that staff were able to react sensitively to children, but there was a lack in the other two types of engagement. However, practitioners showed greater sensitivity, stimulation and autonomy after taking part in the EEL project. Children were measured in terms of their level of 'involvement', which was demonstrated through creativity, persistence, energy, precision and concentration. There were five levels, from low involvement to high.

In conclusion

The way adults behave does affect children and their learning. Staff need to join in with children's play and all activities. Sometimes the adult may need to support reticent children in their play, sometimes they may need to help children use negotiation to solve problems, sometimes they may need to challenge stereotypical play. Their mere presence at an activity raises its status and enhances the self-esteem of the children involved in the activity. Analysis of your work helps to make sure that the whole environment is working in the best way for all children.

8: Modes of learning

Wells (1987) describes children as 'meaning makers'. In one sense or another we are all meaning makers, but at an early age most of life is taken up with trying to make sense of the world. The adults around young children are there to help them to make sense and reach their full potential. This learning for young children will be easy or more difficult depending on the way it is presented.

Children need the means to find out about the world around them, make sense of their discoveries, and discover their culture. They need a mechanism, a mode, a vehicle through which they can make their discoveries and thereby learn. Nursery pioneers suggested that children learnt most easily through movement, play and sensory experience, and in fact highlighted movement as the main mechanism by which young children learnt. These modes of learning are still relevant as they enable children to learn more easily. Using these methods means that discovery and exploration is not a chore but something to relish as they are natural to children.

However, not only are movement, play and sensory experience vehicles for learning, but they also act as learning in themselves; children move to learn but they also learn to move (Gallahue 1989, Davies 1995), they play to learn but also learn to play, they experience to learn but also learn to experience. Similarly children are learning to talk and talking to learn (Wells 1987). But both learning to . . . and . . . to learn are inextricably linked. This chapter will look at how these modes of learning are crucial in helping young children to find out and make sense of their discoveries.

Movement

Movement is probably the most crucial mode of learning for young children. 'Words are at first merely a way of pointing to things, and but empty sounds until the children have had a rich contact with the things themselves, and explored them with hand and eye' (Isaacs 1954, p. 74). She goes on to argue that children need to do and explore to understand meaning, by walking and stretching they come to understand 'far' and 'near' and so on.

> It is important to recognise the role of movement as common denominator of the total development of the child, and its integrating function. Movement is bound up with physical, intellectual, emotional development and a child's doing, thinking and feeling may be examined in movement terms. (Brearley 1969, p. 83)

From birth, children discover through moving themselves about and manipulating materials about them. The prime concerns for a baby are interaction with others and to be in a position to explore, hence the strong drive to reach, sit up, crawl, walk and so on. And so this discovery continues until the three- and four-year-old wants to understand such concepts as 'near and far', 'heavy and light', 'lines and curves' and similar principles. Their own movement and the manipulation of the world around them is their way of finding out about such concepts. For example, 'heavy and light' can be explored through pulling a truck with and without a child in. 'Lines and curves' can be discovered by making these with bricks, blocks or stones. 'Through movement and play, children learn more than motor skills, they learn to employ cognitive strategies, to understand their psychological self and how to interact with other children' (Zaichkowsky *et al.* 1980, p. 11). So children have to learn to crawl, walk and run. Through this movement they can also learn about concepts and they can experiment with ideas, whether mathematical ideas or social ones which involve using the appropriate body language for the particular social situation.

Separating PE from the rest of the activities in school has made sure that the development of body and mind are separate: as though the mind is developed in the classroom and the body through a PE lesson (Boorman 1988). She argues that 'Cognitive, physical and emotional growth need to develop alongside one another – each contributing to the other' (p. 232). This is just as McMillan and the nursery pioneers had argued that both body and mind had to be healthy and that one could not function properly if the other was not healthy.

Matthews (1994), discussing drawing and painting, demonstrates that action and movement are important to thinking and feeling and thereby to visual representation and expression. Matthews shows that a subject such as drawing is not narrow, simply involving pencil and paper. There is a whole process of discovery with all sorts of other materials – anything which children can lay their hands on and that the drawing is a part of that discovery process about the world and how things happen and why. Children will be moving to help with their drawing and drawing to find out about the world. 'When they represent anything (using a mark, a shape, an action or an object) *they make something stand for something else*, and *through expression* (in speech, action or images) *they show emotion*' (p. 9).

Wetton (1998) discusses the lack of movement opportunities within schools now and how children can become frustrated and appear naughty. 'More likely, and almost by way of compensation, the children try to find spaces where they "are allowed to move" – as in life corners where it is acceptable to crawl like a dog or climb to wash windows or pretend to be a dancing Teletubby' (p. 99). More often now than in the past, I see children being told off for such imaginative behaviour and all they are asking is to 'learn by doing'. Activity has been taken away because of the National Curriculum and testing, but movement is essential to young learners.

Movement, and not just physical development

It needs to be appreciated, however, that there is movement and there is physical development; the former is a mode through which children can learn and the latter is one aspect of child development. By movement is meant walking, playing with another child, pulling a truck, building with bricks or walking along a balancing beam, and it is therefore more than just physical development. Movement can be physical, constructive or creative play; enhancing physical development is only one component. This is why outdoors needs to be viewed as a learning and teaching environment, not simply the physical exercise area. One of the reasons the outdoor play area has been pushed to the sidelines is that it has come to be seen as the physical exercise domain, where only physical development is enhanced, and thus is seen as less important than other areas of development, but the place where children run around, kick balls and ride bikes. I am still reading early years textbooks published recently, which discuss outdoor play in the physical development chapter; so-called experts are not aware that outdoor play includes the whole curriculum, not just physical development. It is hardly surprising that staff in early years settings get confused.

With the ranking of development such as can be seen in the Taylor *et al.* study (1972), physical development has come to be seen as less important than other development. The unfortunate consequence of this ranking is that physical development has been confused with movement and so not only has physical activity been demoted, so too a mode of learning has been demoted. But movement as a mode of learning can occur everywhere, in both the indoor and outdoor environments. What the outdoor environment can offer, which indoors cannot, is the space for children to move freely, to move so that they can use their whole bodies in imaginative and fantasy play situations, to grapple with concepts which can more easily be understood and appreciated on a large scale.

Movement and thinking

Bruce (1987), looking at Bruner's theories, argues that the modes of learning for young children are the enactive (action); the iconic (graphic or visual); and the symbolic (abstract). She argues that the active mode is the most developed in young children and the most crucial. 'Most developed' means it is probably the most accessible vehicle for learning. Piaget's notion is that 'thought' is 'internalised action'. Athey (1990) identifies schemas which are patterns of behaviour which are significant in helping children make sense of their world and learning. She argues that through physical activity children can secure information about themselves, the environment and the topological properties of objects, and understand shape, form and movement. Through movement children can find out about space, direction, laterality, dominance. All of these are important with regard to, for example, coping with writing, manipulating tools or crossing the road. Movement is about enabling children to get to grips with things so that they can eventually get to grips with ideas.

> Four-year-old Mario had a truck stacked with crates which were badly arranged and in danger of toppling over. In fact this was exactly what happened when another child crashed into the truck. Mario set to work and tried to stack them in a more orderly fashion but with the addition of the tenth crate they all fell down. Mario decided to take all the crates out of the truck and start from the beginning. He tried the crates so that the maximum surface area of the truck was covered. He eventually worked out that two flat, and one on its side, used the space most effectively. He then very carefully stacked the crates one on top of the other, ensuring they all fitted properly. The stacks got too high and Mario was confused as to what to do to be able to continue stacking. He then decided to use a chair to stand on. Having finally got the thirteen crates into the truck, Mario, *without* moving the truck, realised that the crates balanced on their sides would fall out unless he secured them in some way. He asked the teacher for a rope, and spent some time attaching the rope to the crates on their side and then feeding the rope through and attaching it to the securely standing crates. Mario moved off with the truck and the crates stayed in place. The whole process had taken thirty minutes. (Bilton 1989)

Apart from a brief functional conversation, Mario had not spoken, but this did not mean he had not been thinking. He had solved a number of problems, he had foreseen another. Mario could not have solved the puzzle of fitting 13 crates into a truck if he had been asked to work it out on paper, but through this activity this is what he did.

Fifty per cent of intellectual development occurs in the first five years of life, therefore the majority of mental mapping occurs at this time. The brain has its own timetable and there are critical periods when the brain craves the right experiences. Around the age of three the brain craves understanding and stimulation through curiosity. Each child has to build their own knowledge (Vygotsky 1978). It is, therefore, vital that children are able to access the easiest mode of learning and this can only be done by allowing them to manipulate the environment for themselves. Children cannot learn if someone else is doing the manipulation. Although there is not a causal relationship between developmental coordination disorder (DCD) ('clumsy') and school achievement, there is evidence to suggest there *is* a firm relationship which demonstrates that children who show signs of DCD do less well in school than would have been predicted from their cognitive ability (Sugden and Wright 1996).

Movement and social interaction

Vygotsky (1978), Wells (1987) and Trevarthen (1994) argue that social interaction and communication are central to children's development; they need and want to communicate with other children and adults. Vygotsky demonstrates how socialised speech is internalised by children and structures their thinking and concept formation. Trevarthen demonstrates how important the fantasy world is to children at around the age of four, and how they are clearly able to imitate and act out a story. What is very important at this stage is for children to act out the drama as real people.

This closely parallels Wood's (1988) theory that children are novices, adults being the experts, and so children need to play around with ideas, to be in the expert roles and to 'have a go'. This is about children using themselves as the players in socio-dramatic play. For this role-play, children need space to act out and dramatise. Clearly the outside area offers this space for life-size social interaction and talk, where children can experiment with ideas and states of mind by taking on real roles. Role-play needs to be constantly available, with access to enough props so that when the direction of the play changes children have enough.

Movement and feelings

Movement is clearly linked to emotional development. Brearley (1969) argues that movement 'reflects the inner activity of the person' (p. 88). Through movement children can express their feelings, whether by skipping for joy, running, stamping to let out anger, or walking to get rid of tension. But more than this, success in movement can improve the self-image. Success in movement reinforces children's self-image, how they feel about their body will affect how they feel about themselves (Gallahue 1989). The opposite must, therefore, also hold; that lack of success in movement can lower the self-image. Exercise can raise the mood of a person, lessen anxiety and raise self-esteem in adults also (Fox 1996). He points to the evidence of Calfas and Taylor (1994) with regard to adolescents, and suggests that there is no reason not to assume that these same changes occur in young children and that physical activity affects a child's state of mind. In the Gruber (1986) study, children's self-esteem grew with exercise.

A study by a PE teacher into children with coordination problems found that these problems caused other difficulties, namely lack of confidence and self-esteem, bad behaviour, restlessness, poor handwriting and introversion. By offering these children

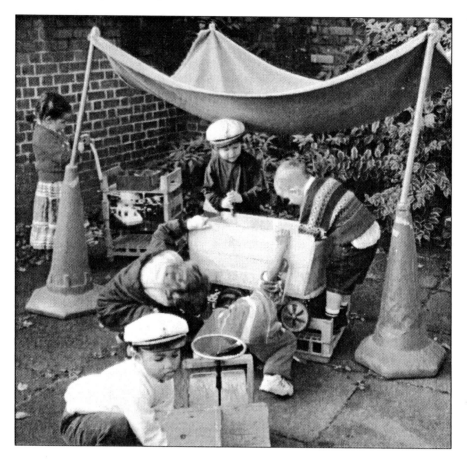

Figure 8.1 A garage – movement and talk linked.

a structured PE programme he found that not only did the children's motor skills and stamina improve but so too did their self-esteem, both in PE and in general class activities (Stewart 1989, p. 32).

If children are given sufficient vigorous activity they are then more ready to work at sedentary activities (Manning and Sharp 1977).

Movement and physical activity

The link between movement and physical activity is obvious. Through movement children learn to refine and improve motor skills, develop their coordination, balance and body awareness, and can keep the body, heart and other organs healthy. What appears to be less obvious is what constitutes physical activity. Over time there has been a change in approach to fitness and exercise. Recently there has been a boom in exercise, health clubs, and the like, with the emphasis changing from exercise to fitness as a lifestyle choice. To some extent this has been mirrored in schools, with a desire for children to take part in exercise sessions. The problem with this is that this type of exercise on its own does not necessarily make a person fit. In the past people were fit because they had to walk to the shops, use a manual lawnmower, wash clothes by hand. However, more recently the emphasis has changed and now the literature suggests that children need to be physically active *per se*, that 'whole body activity' (Jones 1996, p. 52) needs to be fostered, and regular vigorous activity is needed. Physical activity needs to pervade all tasks and involve the whole body, not just parts of it.

Lifestyle

Changes in lifestyle, however, have taken away whole body physical activity; the car means people do not need to walk anywhere. An added problem is that, in the car, children are denied the social contact which was possible before, when walking to school was the norm. Society seems very geared to staying indoors. There is much more television watching, and much computer-based leisure. Technology and gadgets have taken the exercise component out of the chores. Also, parents can be reluctant about allowing children out, even into the street outside the house, either for fear of abduction, or worse, and fear of traffic. Parks and forests where children could go to play, away from adults, are now often out of bounds, unless very close to the house, for the same reasons. Many children live in cramped conditions, with no gardens, where even the local park is out of bounds because it is unhygienic. Others may live in more spacious accommodation but are unable to use the space because of fears of making a mess. Even gardens can be out of bounds because parents do not want their well-tended gardens spoilt.

So the situation is one of many children having no or little access to outdoor areas or outdoor play, who experience little exercise and tend to be sedentary for a good deal of the time. One could say 'so what?', human beings are forever adapting and changing and this change in lifestyle does not matter. However, it matters a great deal and if we do not take care and ensure that children take exercise, then problems are being created for the futures of those children. Physical exercise helps strengthen muscles, improve muscular endurance, increase bone density and flexibility and improve the cardio-respiratory functions. The Allied Dunbar National Fitness Survey (Sports Council 1992) established how little activity is being undertaken by different age groups and that there is a clear association between past participation in sport and physical recreation and the prevalence of breathlessness, angina and heart disease. This research found that activity levels varied according to social and economic status, with those in the lower groups tending to exercise less. Research links adult activity with mental well-being and an absence of ill-health.

Obesity problems in adults in Britain seem to be mirrored in children (Fox 1996). A study of 10- to 16-year-olds found that British children rarely take part in vigorous sustained activity sufficient to optimise their aerobic fitness (Armstrong and Bray 1991). The National Osteoporosis Society found, for young children in particular, that exercise and good calcium intake are two keys to preventing osteoporosis in later life. However, they also noted that this is not happening (Edwards 1992). The need for children to take part in exercise is now being stressed more and more.

Finally, child participation in physical activity is mirrored in adult participation; if children do not get involved in physical activity, it is unlikely they will as adults.

The message is that children need to take part in whole body activity. This does not necessarily mean sport but activities such as walking and moving when playing. They need opportunities for vigorous activity which gives psychological benefit that will carry on into adulthood. Children leading a healthy lifestyle hopefully will mean healthy adults. The European Network of Health Promoting Schools, a research development project, is involving a number of schools in the country in following a health curriculum and so contributing to the health of their community.

In practice

In practice children need to be physically active, whether when playing imaginatively, constructing or taking part in PE-type activities. Young children, therefore, need to be outdoors so that activity is part of their daily routine. Through the imaginative and construction activities of outdoor play, children are not only developing social and linguistic skills, but also strengthening muscles, working heart and lungs and seeing physical activity as a natural component of their day. Children also need opportunities for vigorous activity where they get out of breath, and the heart works faster; this can include simple running games. I have often wondered why young children are so keen to play chase, and have come to the conclusion that they love having fun but also know that something as simple as 'chase' is good for them. So setting up safe chase games is an effective way of ensuring vigorous activity. Games of jumping from one marked spot to another, skipping, or galloping will all achieve the same end. But they also incorporate cooperation, spatial awareness, directional change, and could incorporate counting. All of these games need to be part of the planning process, but such games could be included on an ongoing list, to refer to as you are working outside, similar to a list of songs.

Once taught, children will play these games on their own and make up new ones which will be important not only in the Foundation Stage environment but also in the infant playground. The benefits may not only be seen in terms of healthier children, but also in terms of mental well-being, as suggested in the Manning and Sharp (1977) research. Through this exercise, children can get rid of tension and aggression, which will enable them to settle to any activity, (not necessarily sedentary), which requires a level of concentration.

Children go through specific stages of physical development – initial, elementary and mature – and movement falls into three categories – locomotion, balance and manipulation. By the age of seven all the fundamental skills are in place and it is therefore incumbent upon staff to make sure children have plenty of experience of how to move correctly (Cratty 1986, Gallahue 1989). Children need the experience of large-muscle movements as these develop before the smaller ones and so children need experience of, for example, swinging from a bar and digging, to strengthen arm muscles, which in turn will enable the smaller arm muscles to be used when drawing and writing. The work of Matthews (1988) makes the link between movement and drawing and subsequently writing, and the evidence shows that children need to make particular movements when babies and then as toddlers, to use those movements eventually in drawing.

It is not enough to have a 'sense' about what constitutes movement, it is necessary to know exactly what it is and its component parts (Davies 1995). She classifies movement as being about the body (action, articulation, design, fluency and shape), about dynamics (weight, space (qualitative), time and flow), about space (size, extension, zone, level and direction) and about relationships (between parts of the body, with objects and with people) (pp. 1–2). Just as adults will have a repertoire of ideas, for example, to help children to learn to read, they also need a repertoire of ideas to teach movement skills. Davies details the stages of development, such as the change in throwing technique, from age 18 months (p. 25). With this type of knowledge teachers can really help children to move on in their skill acquisition.

As always, a balance has to be struck between providing skill-based intervention teaching specific points and giving children enough time to be spontaneous and creative. Children need opportunities to try out their bodies and find out what they can do. Movement is about self-discovery, 'What can I do?', 'What can my body do?' If children can experiment and have fun when moving, this can increase their self-respect and self-worth. They will then go on to try new and challenging movements and so the cycle of confidence moves upwards. If children only get periodic experience of something it is unlikely they will move on in their acquisition of skills; they will spend time simply retreading old skills and this can create more chance for accidents and particularly so in outdoor play. Vygotsky's (1978) 'ripening structures' can hardly be catered for if some activities are only provided every other week.

In conclusion, then, through movement children can learn, find out, think through, learn about the world, express and modify feelings, enhance their self-esteem, become fit and healthy, practise the skills of social interaction and develop their language.

Play

Inextricably linked with learning through movement is, of course, play.

> One of the best and easiest pathways to a strong self concept is through play. Play offers opportunities to assist the child in all areas of development. Its importance can be found in how he (the child) perceives himself, his body, his abilities and his relationships with others. (Taylor 1980, p. 133)

Play so easily incorporates all the areas of learning; this can be seen in the pizza delivery play set up (Chapter 7, Figure 7.4). In particular personal, social and emotional development were catered for and the study by Whitehurst (2001) makes a clear link between play, play outside and personal, social and emotional and development. The Foundation Stage guidance suggests that PSE is the most important area of learning. Haines (2000) making a comparison between nursery education in Denmark and England discusses a Danish study about why outside environments seem so beneficial to children. This argues that it is due to the positive attitude of staff to outside, who consider playing outside is more beneficial than time spent inside and that play outside gives children opportunities for social and emotional development that cannot be found elsewhere. Katz (1995) discussing self-esteem, a very central aspect of PSE development, argues that much of the practices 'intended to enhance it are more likely to foster preoccupation with oneself and with the way one appears to others' (p. 43). She argues that self-esteem is achieved through helping children to cope with frustrations and negative comments rather than going over the top with praise and flattery. She argues that self-confidence comes from making children competent, creating a learning environment where children are able to make proper decisions, where they can make real choices and have interesting challenge rather than quick success. Her discussions make for powerful reading and demonstrate that some of what is put out and done for children in the name of help is incredibly low level intellectually and sometimes an insult, which Katz describes as 'frivolous and cute' (p. 40). Quality play engages children because although it is not real to us, it is as real as they can get – they can pretend it's a real fire without getting burnt. During play children will come across other children as say mothers saying not very nice things, shopkeepers being unhelpful, planks getting stuck in an A-frame and they then have to make real decisions as to what to do and what to say. Adults find play difficult because it is children's real world but not theirs. What do we feel when children want to come into our adult real world? Sometimes we are pleased, sometimes we just want to get on, sometimes we feel pushed out, but mostly we want to be in control. These are the emotions children feel in their real world of play. We must give it more credit.

Play is also an easy means of learning for young children, as they are naturally drawn to it and want to get involved in it. They often seem most at ease when in a play situation and Lally (1991) talks in terms of play being the 'perfect vehicle' (p. 72) because children are naturally motivated through it. She suggests that play can offer children opportunities to 'explore and discover, construct, repeat and consolidate, represent, create, imagine, socialise' (pp. 72–4).

When social interaction and talk are discussed, play quite naturally comes into the equation. And just as children need to be taught *how* to play they can also learn through the mechanism of play. Singer and Singer (1990) indicate the centrality of dramatic play to young children's development, and Smilansky and Shefatya (1990) argue that children who can readily manipulate symbols in dramatic play are more likely to accept and use the arbitrary symbols of mathematics and written language.

One of the important components of playing is that it involves others; it tends to be social. One of the primary functions of play is to develop children's language and social skills (Wood and Bennett 1997) and this neatly fits with ideas expressed concerning children learning through movement. Imaginative play and constructional play tend to be social. Kitson (1994) details the importance of socio-dramatic play for learning. Frost and Campbell (1985) found that children aged four to six preferred an environment which encouraged dramatic play.

Through role-play, children are able to decentre (Bruce 1987), to see something from another perspective and this is crucial for a society to function well. Children cannot find out what it is like to see something from another perspective unless they can get into that person's shoes. What the outdoors affords to young children is the opportunity to be in role, to be playing imaginatively, and more than this, it enables them to be involved in fairly large groups. This is not only because there is more space, and noise is more easily dissipated outside, but also because there is a greater sense of freedom in the outdoors.

Linking with the original ideas put forward in Chapter 1 on management and organisation, the important issues concerning play outside are that:

- children know they have time and space to play,
- they will not be interrupted,
- they can control the environment themselves, and
- they know they can bring anything within reason into the play scene, including people.

The following scene may go some way to explaining these ideas.

> Robert, Barry and Matthew parked three wooden trucks containing milk crates next to the school. The children, by their actions, had obviously decided this was the milk depot. One of Robert's crates fell off. 'Oh, I must have been going too fast.' 'I've got more than you,' said Matthew. He then counted his crates and also Robert's. 'You've got more.' The teacher, when she entered the scene, was told: 'We're delivering milk. We leave the trucks this way' (Robert gestured) 'at night, and then turn them round in the morning.' Two other children joined the group. The teacher asked if she could buy some milk. 'Yes, and there's bread also,' said Robert. A discussion ensued about how much milk and bread was wanted, and the price and then 'goods and money' exchanged hands. The children went off. They returned to the teacher three minutes later. 'You need some more bread, milk and . . . a present,' said Robert. 'I've got peas and veg,' said Matthew. The teacher and two other children bought bread and milk and the teacher took the present. Robert then tried to take Matthew's black crate which was the bread crate. An argument began and the teacher became involved. Suddenly, Matthew shouted, 'The bread's been stolen!' 'You need to go to the police station to report it,' replied the teacher. 'The police have stolen it,' Matthew declared. All the children involved laughed and the disagreement was forgotten. Scott joined the group. 'I've bought some shopping, here you are,' he said, and gave it to the teacher. 'It's ever so heavy,' replied the teacher. 'It cost one,' Scott said. The teacher gave him 'one'. Naomi joined the group. 'Can I buy some milk?' Robert replied, 'No! You can have it delivered this afternoon. Go home and wait.' Naomi went. By this time Matthew had moved away from the group and was lying on the ground mending his truck. As the teacher moved towards him he shouted, 'It's fixed,' and went off towards Robert. 'I've got fruit for sale,' said Matthew, and they went off together. (Bilton 1989, pp. 40–1)

This play scene carried on for an hour and involved various children moving in and out of the play. Significant in this scene is the length of time it continued and that children were able to continue the play, despite difficulties they faced in it.

Having time to play

In this scene children could get on and play, on what was a very cold day, but they were wrapped up warmly, they were moving and so kept warm, and there were no interruptions or distractions to their play. The significance of play to children is shown by their desire to continue it and the skills they employ to continue it. In the scene where Robert added a present to the second transaction with the teacher, it may be that he just wanted to add a present. But it may have been added to encourage the teacher to join in the play. The teacher had already bought milk and bread and may not have wanted to buy more, a present would be an added incentive. Matthew successfully defused the argument over the crate – which could have easily brought the game to a halt – by saying the crate had been stolen. Matthew also showed that he knew where he wanted the play to go, by rejecting the teacher's suggestion that they should go to the police station to report that the bread had been stolen; he countered by saying the police had stolen it. He was obviously wanting to be in control of the play and knew how he wanted the play to unfold. By telling Naomi to go home and wait for the bread to be delivered, Robert was extending the play and creating a scene where the children had to travel, rather than stay still.

Children will exercise great self-control and will bow to the rules of the game in meaningful play situations, so the game is not stopped or spoilt and through this play higher-order functioning occurs (Vygotsky 1978). Play offers a meaningful context for children and it is only when a situation has meaning and purpose that children can function at a higher level (Donaldson 1978).

These children knew they had time to play, they had space and resources and so the play could function on a complicated level. One of the reasons children need time to play is that they need time to initially jostle for position, get into the play scene. Equally children cannot concentrate and show they can persevere if they are interrupted. Play can only work well if it is given time to develop. Some play can only be classified as mundane and rather pointless because children have been given no time to do much else with it.

Controlling the environment for play

The following scene looks at how children control their play. The staff had set up a train scene outside using hollow blocks, a steering wheel, and an assortment of hats, whistles, batons and bags. Four children entered the scene and started to put on the hats, pick up bags and arrange themselves on the blocks. This scene lasted some minutes and seemed to be the time when the children were getting into role and playing with where the scene was to go. Two other children joined and wanted to set up a café on the train. They disappeared to get milk crates and pieces of flat wood. These they arranged to act as cooker, sink, worktops and so on. They disappeared again to get cups, plates and saucepans, plus sticks and leaves for the food. The hollow blocks then had string tied on for seat belts which caused a heated discussion about whether trains had seat belts. This was then followed by a scene of people being on a

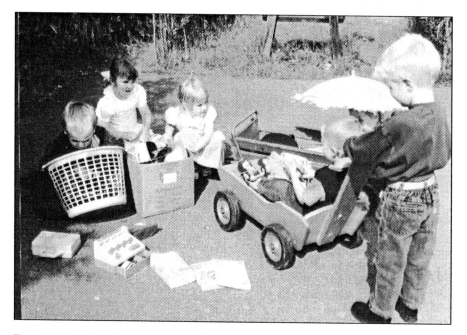

Figure 8.2 Starting off – negotiating and thinking about where the play could go.

train, buying food, eating it, and moving about the train. One child who had been in the scene returned with a piece of material for a bed and a bag filled with various items for his journey.

These children could not have reached this detail or level of play if they had not been allowed to adapt the original set-up and use equipment to suit their needs, for example, the crates for kitchen equipment. Children need to use their imaginations and to control, modify and change their environment. Only in this way can play between children develop; and it is when it develops, that really imaginative play comes in. A ready-made environment with fixed climbing frames and painted vehicle lines cannot be controlled because it gives little scope for children to add to or change. When children are able to control their environment their behaviour changes (Ranzoni 1973). A changeable environment encourages knowledge-seeking behaviour, interest, and extends exploration (Overholser and Pellerin 1980).

Equally, materials which are too representative or that represent only one thing do not allow children to use their imaginations fully. Children need simple yet versatile resources and equipment which they can adapt to suit their needs and level of understanding. These children also knew they could use materials from any learning area for their purposes, that they could move in and out of areas for the play. It is very hard to extend play and develop ideas if only seven dinosaurs and five stones are put in the sand, with no option to use any other resources. No wonder some staff shy away from playing with children!

Children will not always need actual resources to represent something, for example, in the scene with the milkmen, milk, bread, a present and money were all in the players' imaginations. But equally, children may want to make the resources. The trick is to not only to get children to build with blocks and crates and material to create a structure they want, but also to use the materials from the technology table to make what they need. So, if children need binoculars they can make them, if they need maps they can make them, if they want instruments attached to themselves for a band-playing scene they can make them.

How to organise imaginative play

Children will either devise their own play scenes and friends to play with or they will use the play scene devised by the staff. Both are needed in any Foundation Stage setting. For any play to work there needs to be an environment in which to play, which children can control, in which an ethos has been created that play is valued, and resources and equipment available to play with.

The staff can set-up play scenes, alongside free-play scenes, for example the pizza delivery scene mentioned in the planning sheet (Chapter 7, Figure 7.4). The staff and children devised this. Plans were drawn up as to what learning might occur, what resources and equipment were needed and what children could make themselves. Then children started to make pretend pizzas and garlic breads, design and eventually make and mass-produce logos and labels. Menus were written and rewritten and telephones made. With this came lots of talk about fast food and home deliveries. Then equipment was gathered and parents were involved in collecting things. Then a counter was made and stocked and children started to use it. The bikes were transformed to be the delivery vehicles and were used. Staff acted out scenes that might occur in the shop and on the phone. Books were used to open discussions about the subject. And so, gently, the whole pizza delivery scene was opened.

Often play areas are changed overnight and children are expected to immediately fall into playing a new role. They have had no help or ideas given. Some children do not need a stimulus, but some do. Therefore, it is important to build up to a play scene and provide ideas. Sometimes it is fun to change an area overnight but this shouldn't happen all the time. The beauty of the approach above is that it gives children time to think about it. Over time the pizza delivery was added to. Maps were made, foods, menus and so on had to be remade as supplies got used up or broken. Children devised their own play scenes within this broad scene.

Staff initially set up 'homes' from A-frames, material, bricks and blocks for deliveries to be made to. Children then built their own houses, and each day play either continued from the day before, or started again.

Children were able to think and were made to think for themselves, solving problems within the play. Children needed to cooperate, negotiate, interact in different ways. Staff incorporated maths work into the scenes, regarding prices, totals, quantities and so on. Staff and children were involved in long and complicated conversations. Lots of movement of various types were involved in the play – including using the bikes, packing the boxes, manoeuvring about the counter.

A lot of work went into planning and setting up this play scene, but it was worth it as children were able to think, discuss, be responsible, concentrate, persist, represent.

Teaching and play

The teaching component of play can sometimes be explicit and sometimes implicit. When staff are fine-tuning the environment they are making sure that children's play can be concentrated and detailed. It may involve bringing in a teaching point by adding resources which make the children face a new concept. The teaching component to play may involve simply being in role and developing language or using counting, linking work done through a matching game, for example.

But the teaching component can be more explicit. By making the resources for their play, children can put to good use skills gained elsewhere and staff can help. So, when children make the musical instruments for their street-band scene, they will be designing, estimating, counting, cutting, writing.

Encouraging children to talk about their play may be a key teaching component of play and Bennett *et al.* (1997) suggest this needs to be recognised. A discussion or review time needs careful handling and planning but may mean that children could 'become more consciously aware of what they are doing, learning and achieving in their play' (Bennett *et al.* 1997, p. 130). This could be incorporated into a general whole group time and will clearly have links to both language and mathematical development.

Play can seem somewhat divorced from anything else that is going on in the class. To consolidate ideas children need to express them in some way, and talking is one means by which they can express themselves. It will not be possible to have every child discussing their play every day but it should be possible to cover a class, in, say, a week. Bringing play to a forum may raise its status and raise the status of those involved. Children could be asked to tell the story of . . . and be asked what they have learnt, whether they want the play to continue and where they want the play to lead the next day. They could also be asked to focus on a particular aspect of the play, maybe tell a story. This means children need to be clear, logical and reflective. The learning potential of such times is high: the teaching possibilities are there. But there is also the benefit of staff being able to assess what children have learnt and assess the potential of the play.

Sensory experience

We are born with five senses through which we receive input from outside ourselves: sight, hearing, touch, taste, smell. Children need to use these senses to discover and explore, but they also need to learn how to use them. Children need help to focus in on each sense and so use it effectively, and teachers have many activities, for example to develop children's ability to listen.

Intrinsically linked to sensory experience is emotion. We cannot appreciate the beauty of a scent or sight without engaging our emotions. Looking and listening are not just about the gathering of facts, some experiences can bring out certain emotions. Children need to have experiences which heighten emotions such as wonder, joy and excitement, and children need adults who will use the natural resources to bring out and develop these emotions. The relevance of discussing this in a book about outdoor play is that the outdoor area lends itself to teaching through the senses and making children more aware of them. Thus, by using natural resources outside children can be taught so much about the basic concepts of size, shape, number and so on which are part and parcel of everyday school teaching.

> In the school garden there were four logs, used for studying minibeasts. On this particular day, Harpreet and Hardeep had pushed the log over and been confronted by a three-inch stag beetle. Immediately other children gathered round to have a look. Initially, children and teacher just watched. The teacher suggested no one should touch the beetle so that it would not rush away or get hurt and just in case it tried to bite someone. The first topic of conversation was its size, and this was compared to the centipedes, wood lice and ants which were moving about. This then led onto a discussion that the centipede was more 'fluffy' and had more legs than the beetle. The beetle continued to be still. When it did move, the reaction from the children was one of utmost surprise and delight. The teacher suggested the children should move back slightly so that the beetle had space to move about and was not in danger of being stepped on. (Bilton 1989, p. 46)

In this situation the teacher was making sure the children were patient, for to learn from such experience it is necessary to wait and watch. This was an emotional experience, children were delighted, they were curious, they had a sense of wonder. Through patience children were able to learn about the stag beetle and appreciate and learn about its size, texture, shape and number of legs and antennae. Further learning could be through drawing and talking about the experience.

Richards (1983) talks in terms of 'active exploration of the world outdoors' (p. 101). He talks about children being able to touch, lift, handle, feel things while not being able to see the objects. And through this type of experience they can try to distinguish and describe different textures, shapes, even the temperature and movement of things. He talks in terms of using the sense of smell to distinguish pleasant, unpleasant, country, city, household and garden smells. Children can be encouraged to smell the difference between dandelions, marigolds and pansies. Copying colour matches from nature can bring out interesting discussions, for example, red dots on white or yellow stripes on black. This isolation of a sense, as in the example of getting children to experience through touch and hearing but not sight, or asking children to pick out sounds without looking, enables children to focus in on each sense and thereby develop it. These types of experiences encourage children to be aware, to notice, listen, be interested in everything around them.

The garden is an ideal environment to enable children to develop and use their senses and to hone one particular sense. A herb garden does not take much effort to make and yet children can be taught not only to experience the different smells, but also to describe them, compare them and ultimately use them in cooking. Flowers are ideal for sensory experiences, they can be looked at, smelt, felt and some can be tasted. Proper study of flowers, stems, leaves, seeds, and bark can lead to excellent comparative work and a true appreciation of such things as colour and texture. In case study 2 (Chapter 2) the teacher had easily set up various small areas for different sensory experiences, which children could access themselves or a teacher could utilise for a teaching point. She had a sight area with mirrors and reflective materials, a hearing section with chimes, scented herbs and flowers were planted for the smelling area and for touch there were various different textured stones, barks and shells.

Part of the work outside will be devoted to sensory experience, particularly that in the horticultural and scientific areas. Staff need to set up activities which focus children's attention on using their senses to make discoveries. Sensory stimulation fits well with this age, as this is a time when curiosity is at its peak.

In conclusion

Movement, play and sensory experience are vehicles through which young children can learn easily. Children not only need plenty of experiences so that they learn *how* to move, *how* to play, and *how* to use their senses but also a range of experiences so that they learn *through* movement, play and the senses.

9: Epilogue

I will always remember one warm Monday morning in Hackney when Darren's Mum rushed in and said, 'Darren writted his name. You didn't teach him, I didn't teach him!' I took this as a compliment. Darren and his friend Jason played almost exclusively in the garden, but used the indoors when they needed resources for their outdoor play. Darren had used the outdoor area in the way described in this book and he managed to 'writ' his name at four and a half years of age. His Mum had seen me play and work with Darren in a learning and teaching environment, so she did not consider I had formally taught him.

Indoors, and outdoors, together make a complete nursery learning and teaching environment. By the time Darren left to go to infant school his Mum knew the power of outdoor play.

Making changes to practice has to be about taking small steps, many of which this book covers, but with such small steps, big leaps can be made.

Appendix: Useful contacts

1. Learning through Landscapes (LTL), Third Floor, Southside Offices, The Law Courts, Winchester, SO23 9DL
Tel: 01962 846258 *schoolgrounds–uk@ltl.org.uk*

This is the national school grounds charity and it will give help, advice and information on any aspect of the school grounds. They can offer information about good practice and possible sources of funding. They also provide legal and technical advice as well as training, and they produce books and pamphlets. This charity's work deals with all school age groups but does not cover all that is relevant to the outdoor area for three to fives.

2. Local contacts

Your local authority will have a contact person with regard to safety issues. Some local authorities may have a contact person for the Countryside Management Service, who can offer advice about improving the school grounds and possible sources of funding. Sawmills, country parks, forestry departments, etc. may be able to help with providing log sections and wooden boxes.

3. RoSPA, Edgbaston Park, 353 Bristol Road, Birmingham, B5 7ST
Tel: 0121 248 2000 *www.rospa.com*
Playground office: 3 Earning Street, Godmanchester, Cambs, PE29 2JD
Tel: 01480 411384 email: *www.rospaplaysafety.co.uk*

The Royal Society for the Prevention of Accidents have useful publications regarding safety, risk assessment, standards, but be aware none directly relate to educational settings.

4. Community Playthings, Robertsbridge, East Sussex, TN32 5DR
Tel: 0800 387457 *www.communityplaythings.com*

A supplier of very well-made and long-lasting equipment for all aspects of play – imaginative, physical, constructive. In particular, they have playcubes, carriages, wheelbarrows, blocks – unit and hollow.

5. Brian Clegg, Slackcote Mill, Slackcote Lane, Delph, Oldham, OL3 5TP
Tel: 01457 875881

A-frames, ladders, trucks, pushchairs for children, storage trolleys.

6. GLS Educational Supplies Limited
Tel: 020 8805 8333 *sales@glsed.co.uk*

A-frames, ladders, planks, bars.

7. NES Arnold, Novara House, Excelsior Road, Ashby Park, Ashby de la Zouch, Leicestershire, LE65 1NG
Tel: 0870 600 0192 *www.nesarnold.co.uk*

A-frames, ladders, planks, poles, parallel bars, hay carts, mats.

8. WESCO, 114 Highfields Road, Wilham, Essex, CM8 2HH
Tel: 01376 503590 *www.wesco-group.com*

Ropes, balancing ropes, motor education kits, balls.

9. Galt Educational, Johnsonbrook Road, Hyde, Cheshire, SK14 4QT
Tel: 0870 242 4477 *enquires@galt-educational.co.uk*

Trolleys, mats, plastic cushions, climbing trestle, ladders, cubes, barrels, circle cart, trucks/wagon, balls, hoops.

Bibliography

Anning, A. (1994) 'Play and legislated curriculum. Back to basics: an alternative view', in Moyles, J. R. (ed.) *The Excellence of Play*, 67–75. Buckingham: Open University Press.

Armstrong, N. and Bray, S. (1991) 'Physical activity patterns defined by heart rate monitoring', *Archives of Disease in Childhood* **66,** 245–7.

Athey, C. (1990) *Extending Thought in Young Children. A Parent–Teacher Partnership.* London: Paul Chapman Publishing.

Avery, J. G. and Jackson, R. H. (1993) *Children and Their Accidents.* London: Edward Arnold.

Ball, C. (1994) *Start Right: The Importance of Early Learning.* London: The Royal Society for the Encouragement of Arts, Manufactures and Commerce.

Barbour, A. (1999) 'The impact of playground design on the play behaviors of children with differing levels of physical competence', *Early Childhood Research Quarterly* **14**(1), 75–98.

Barrett, G. (1986) *Starting School: An Evaluation of the Experience.* London: Assistant Masters and Mistresses Association.

Bartholomew, L. (1996) 'Working in a team', in Robson, S. and Smedley, S. (eds) *Education in Early Childhood,* 47–55. London: David Fulton Publishers.

Bates, B. (1996) 'Like rats in a rage', *The Times Educational Supplement* **2**, 20 September, 11.

Bennett, N., Wood, L., Rogers, S. (1997) *Teaching Through Play. Teachers' Thinking and Classroom Practice.* Buckingham: Open University Press.

Bergard, R. (1995) 'Building for Children: The Frankfurt Nursery Building Programme.' Lecture given at the Royal Institute of British Architects, 4 December.

Bilton, H. (1989) *The Development and Significance of the Nursery Garden and Outdoor Play.* Unpublished MA dissertation, University of Surrey.

Bilton, H. (1993) 'The nursery class garden – problems associated with working in the outdoor environment and their possible solutions', *Early Child Development and Care* **93**, 15–33.

Bilton, H. (1994) 'The nursery class garden: designing and building an outdoor environment for young children', *Early Years* **14**(2), 34–7.

Blackstone, T. (1971) *A Fair Start. The Provision of Pre-School Education.* London: Allen Lane The Penguin Press.

Blatchford, P. (1989) *Playtime in the Primary School. Problems and Improvements.* Windsor: NFER-Nelson.

Blenkin, G. M. and Whitehead, M. (1988) 'Creating a context for development', in Blenkin, G. M. and Kelly, A. V. (eds) *Early Childhood Education. A Developmental Curriculum,* 32–60. London: Paul Chapman Publishing.

Board of Education (1905) *Reports on Children Under Five Years of Age in Public Elementary Schools by Women Inspectors of the Board of Education.* London: HMSO.

Board of Education (1912) *Statistics.* Table 3(b). London: HMSO.

Board of Education (1936) *Nursery Schools and Nursery Classes.* London: HMSO.

Boorman, P. (1988) 'The contributions of physical activity to development in the early years', in Blenkin, G. M. and Kelly, A. V. (eds) *Early Childhood Education. A Developmental Curriculum,* 231–250. London: Paul Chapman Publishing.

Bradburn, E. (1976) *Margaret McMillan. Framework and Expansion of Nursery Education.* Redhill: Denholm House Press.

Brearley, M. (ed.) (1969) *Fundamentals in the First School.* Oxford: Blackwell.

Brown, J. G. and Burger, C. (1984) 'Playground designs and preschool children's behaviors', *Environment and Behavior* **16**(5), 599–626.

Bruce, T. (1987) *Early Childhood Education.* London: Hodder & Stoughton.

Burstall, E. (1997) 'Unappreciated and underpaid', *Times Educational Supplement* **2**, 14 February, 13.

Calfas, K. J. and Taylor, W. C. (1994) 'Effect of physical activity on psychological variables in adolescents', *Paediatric Exercise Science* **6**, 406–23.

Clark, M. M. (1988) *Children Under Five: Educational Research and Evidence*. London: Gordon and Breach.

Cleave, S. and Brown, S. (1989) *Four Year Olds in School. Meeting their Needs*. Slough: National Foundation for Educational Research.

Cleave, S. and Brown, S. (1991) *Early to School. Four Year Olds in Infant Classes*. Windsor: NFER-NELSON Publishing.

Cole, E. S. (1990) 'An experience in Froebel's garden', *Childhood Education* **67**(1), 18–21.

Cook, B. and Heseltine, P. (1999) *Assessing Risk on Children's Playgrounds*, 2nd edn. Birmingham: RoSPA.

Cooper, M. and Johnson, A. (1991) *Poisonous Plants and Fungi – An Illustrated Guide*. London: HMSO.

Costello, P. J. M. (2000) *Thinking Skills and Early Childhood Education*. London: David Fulton Publishers.

Cratty, B. J. (1986) *Perceptual and Motor Development in Infants and Children*, 3rd edn. New Jersey: Prentice Hall.

Cullen, J. (1993) 'Preschool children's use and perceptions of outdoor play areas', *Early Child Development and Care* **89**, 45–56.

Cusden, P. E. (1938) *The English Nursery School*. London: Kegan Paul, Trench, Trubner.

Davies, J. (1991) 'Children's adjustment to nursery class: how to equalise opportunities for a successful experience', *School Organisation* **11**(3), 255–62.

Davies, J. and Brember, I. (1994) 'Morning and afternoon nursery sessions: can they be equally effective in giving children a positive start to school?', *International Journal of Early Years Education* **2**(2), 43–53.

Davies, M. (1995) *Helping Children to Learn Through a Movement Perspective*. London: Hodder & Stoughton.

de Lissa, L. (1939) *Life in the Nursery School*. London: Longmans, Green and Co.

Dombey, H. (1993) '"And, they went, they lived there after": making written narrative accessible in the nursery class to children whose cultures don't embrace it', *Changing Education* **1**(1), 141–53.

Donaldson, M. (1978) *Children's Minds*. London: Collins/Fontana.

Dowling, M. (1992) *Education 3–5*, 2nd edn. London: Paul Chapman Publishing.

Dudek, M. (1996) *Kindergarten Architecture*. London: Chapman and Hall.

Dunn, S. and Morgan, V. (1987) 'Nursery and infant school play patterns: sex-related differences', *British Educational Research Journal* **13**(3), 271–81.

Dunne, E. and Bennett, N. (1990) *Talking and Learning in Groups*. London: Routledge.

Edwards, L. (1992) 'Osteoporosis: the fight for recognition', *Nestlé Worldview* **1**(1), 8.

Esbensen, S. B. (1987) *The Early Childhood Playground. An Outdoor Classroom*. Ypsilanti, MI: The High/Scope Press.

Fisher, J. (1996) *Starting from the Child?* Buckingham: Open University Press.

Fox, K. (1996) 'Physical Activity Promotion and the Active School', in Armstrong, N. (ed.) *New Directions in Physical Education. Change and Innovation*, 94–109. London: Cassell.

Frost, J. L. (1986) 'Children's playgrounds', in Fein, G. and Rivkin, M. (eds) *The Young Child at Play – Reviews of Research*, Vol. 4. Washington, DC: National Association for the Education of Young Children.

Frost, J. L. (1992) 'Reflections on research and practice in outdoor play environments', *Dimensions* **20**(3), 6–10.

Frost, J. L. and Campbell, S. D. (1985) 'Equipment choices of primary aged children on conventional and creative playgrounds', in Frost, J. L. and Sunderlin, S. (eds) *When Children Play. Proceedings of the International Conference on Play and Play Environments*, 89–101. Wheaton, MD: Association for Childhood Education International.

Gallahue, D. L. (1989) *Understanding Motor Development. Infants, Children, Adolescents,* 2nd edn. Indianapolis: Benchmark Press.

Galton, M., Simon, B., Croll, P. (1980) *Inside the Primary Classroom.* London: Routledge and Kegan Paul.

Gilkes, J. (1987) *Developing Nursery Education.* Milton Keynes: Open University Press.

Great Britain. House of Commons, Education, Science and Arts Committee (1988) *Educational Provision for the Under Fives: First Report from the Education, Science and Arts Committee,* session 1988–9, **II.** London: HMSO.

Great Britain. Department of Education and Science. (1989) *Aspects of Primary Education. The Education of Children Under Five.* Her Majesty's Inspectorate. London: HMSO.

Great Britain. Department for Education and Employment (1996) *Schools' Environmental Assessment Method (SEAM)* London: The Stationery Office.

Gruber, J. J. (1986) 'Physical activity and self-esteem development in children: A meta analysis', *American Academy of Physical Education Papers* **19**, 30–48.

Gura, P. (1992) *Exploring Learning: Young Children and Blockplay.* London: Paul Chapman.

Haines, J. S. (2000) 'What's in the garden? A comparative study of philosophies in English and Danish nursery settings and their influence on the use of the outside environment'. Unpublished Advanced Diploma, Homerton College.

Halliday, J., McNaughton, S., Glynn, T. (1985) 'Influencing children's choice of play activities at kindergarten through teacher participation', *New Zealand Journal of Educational Studies* **20**(1), 48–58.

Hart, R. (1978) 'Sex differences in the use of outdoor space', in Sprung, B. (ed.) *Perspectives on Non-Sexist Early Childhood Education,* 101–9. New York: Teachers' College Press.

Hartley, D. (1993) *Understanding the Nursery School.* London: Cassell.

Henniger, M. L. (1985) 'Preschool children's play behaviors in an indoor and outdoor environment', in Frost, J. L. and Sunderlin, S. (eds) *When Children Play. Proceedings of the International Conference on Play and Play Environments,* 145–9. Wheaton, MD: Association for Childhood Education International.

Henniger, M. L. (1993/4) 'Enriching the outdoor play experience', *Childhood Education* **V**, 87–90.

Hill, P. (1978) *Play Spaces for Preschoolers: Design Guidelines for the Development of Preschool Play Spaces in Residential Environments.* Ottawa, Canada: Central Mortage and Housing Corporation, National Office.

Hilsum, S. and Cane, B. S. (1971) *The Teacher's Day.* Slough: National Foundation for Educational Research.

Holmes, B. M. and Davies, M. G. (1937) *Organized Play in the Infant and Nursery School.* London: University of London Press.

Hutt, C. (1972) *Males and Females.* Harmondsworth: Penguin Education.

Hutt, S. *et al.* (1989) *Play, Exploration and Learning: A Natural History of the Pre-School.* London: Routledge.

Isaacs, S. (1932) *The Nursery Years.* London: Routledge and Kegan Paul.

Isaacs, S. (1954) *The Educational Value of the Nursery School.* London: The Nursery School Association.

Johnson, J. E., Christie, J. F. and Yawkey, T. D. (1987) *Play and Early Childhood Development.* Glenview, IL: Scott Foresman, and Company.

Jones, C. (1996) 'Physical education at key stage 1', in Armstrong, N. (ed.) *New Directions in Physical Education. Change and Innovation,* 48–61. London: Cassell.

Jordan, E. (1995) 'Fighting boys and fantasy play: The construction of masculinity in the early years of school', *Gender and Education* **7**(1), 69–86.

Katz, L. (1995) *Talks with Teachers of Young Children.* New Jersey: Ablex Publishing Corporation.

Kitson, N. (1994) '"Please Miss Alexander, will you be the robber?" Fantasy play: a case for adult intervention', in Moyles, J. R. (ed.) *The Excellence of Play,* 88–98. Buckingham: Open University Press.

Klein, R. (1997) 'Let the children decide', *The Times Educational Supplement* **2**, 31 October, 12.

Kostelnik, M. J., Whiten, A. P., Stein, L. C. (1986) 'Living with he-man: managing super-hero fantasy play', *Young Children* **41**(4), 3–9.

Kounin, J. S. (1970) *Discipline and Group Management in Classrooms.* New York: Holt, Rinehart and Wilson.

Lally, M. (1991) *The Nursery Teacher in Action.* London: Paul Chapman Publishing.

Lally, M. and Hurst, V. (1992) 'Assessment in nursery education: a review of approaches', in Blenkin, G. M. and Kelly, A. V. (eds) Assessment in Early Childhood Education, 69–92. London : Paul Chapman Publishing.

Lasenby, M. (1990) *The Early Years. A Curriculum for Young Children. Outdoor Play.* London: Harcourt Brace Jovanovich.

Lindberg, L. and Swedlow, R. (1985) *Young Children: Exploring and Learning.* Boston, MA: Allyn and Bacon.

Macintyre, C. (2001) *Enhancing Learning through Play.* London: David Fulton Publishers.

Manning, K. and Sharp, A. (1977) *Structuring Play in the Early Years at School.* London: Ward Lock Educational.

Matthews, J. (1988) 'The young child's early representation and drawing', in Blenkin, G. M. and Kelly, A.V. (eds) *Early Childhood Education. A Developmental Curriculum*, 162–183. London: Paul Chapman Publishing.

Matthews, J. (1994) *Helping Children to Draw and Paint in Early Childhood.* London: Hodder and Stoughton.

McAuley, H. and Jackson, P. (1992) *Educating Young Children. A Structural Approach.* London: David Fulton Publishers.

Mcintyre, C. (2001) *Enhancing Learning through Play.* London: David Fulton.

McLean, S. V. (1991) *The Human Encounter: Teachers and Children Living Together in Preschools.* London: Falmer Press.

McMillan, M. (1919) 'Nursery Schools', *The Times Educational Supplement*, 13 February, 81.

McMillan, M. (1930) *The Nursery School.* London: Dent and Sons.

McNee, D. (1984) 'Outdoor play in the nursery – a neglected area?', *Early Years* **4**(2), 16–25.

Meadows, S. and Cashdan, A. (1988) *Helping Children Learn. Contributions to a Cognitive Curriculum.* London: David Fulton Publishers.

Millard, E. (1997) *Differently Literate: Boys, Girls and the Schooling of Literacy.* London: Falmer Press.

Miller, P. (1972) *Creative Outdoor Play Areas.* New Jersey: Prentice Hall.

Miller, S. (1978) *The Facilitation of Fundamental Motor Skill Learning in Young Children.* Unpublished doctoral dissertation. Michigan State University.

Morgan, V. and Dunn, S. (1990) 'Management strategies and gender differences in nursery and infant classrooms', *Research in Education* **44**, 81–91.

Moyles, J. R. (1992) *Organizing for Learning in the Primary Classroom.* Buckingham: Open University Press.

Nash, B. (1981) 'The effects of classroom spatial organisation on four- and five-year-old children's learning', *British Journal of Educational Psychology* **51**, 144–55.

Naylor, H. (1985) 'Outdoor play and play equipment', *Early Child Development and Care* **19**, 109–30.

Neill, S. (1982) 'Open plan or divided space in pre-school', *Education 3–13* **10**, Autumn, 45–8.

Neumark, V. (1997) 'Father and son reunion', *The Times Educational Supplement* **2**, 13 June, 6.

Noble, C., Brown, J. and Murphy, J. (2001) *How to Raise Boys' Achievement.* London: David Fulton Publishers.

O'Sullivan, J. (1997) 'A bad way to educate boys', *The Independent*, Education+, 3 April, 8–9.

Ouvry, M. (2000) *Exercising Muscles and Minds: Outdoor Play and the Early Years Curriculum.* London: The National Early Years Network.

Overholser, K. M. and Pellerin, D. M. (1980) *An In-service Program in the Area of Children's Outdoor Gross Motor Playground Considerations, Design and Apparati, for the National Association for the Education of Young Children's 1980 Conference Attendees.* Conference paper, Annual meeting of the National Association for the Education of Young Children, San Francisco, 21–4 November.

Owen, G. (1928, rev. edn.) *Nursery School Education.* London: Methuen.

Paley, V. G. (1984) *Boys and Girls: Superheroes in the Doll Corner.* Chicago: The University of Chicago Press.

Paley, V. G. (1986) 'On listening to what children say', *Harvard Educational Review* **56**(2), 122–31.

Parkin, J. (1997) 'Boys and girls come out to play', *The Times Educational Supplement, Extra*, 13 June, VI.

Pascal, C., Bertram. T. and Ramsden, F. (1997) 'The effective early learning research project: reflections upon the action during phase 1', *Early Years* **17**(2), 40–7.

Plaisted, L. (1909) *The Early Education of Children.* Oxford: Oxford University at the Clarendon Press.

Pollard, A. and Tann, S. (1987) *Reflective Teaching in the Primary School.* London: Cassell.

Pound, L. (1987) 'The nursery tradition', *Early Child Development and Care* **28**, 79–88.

QCA, (2000) *Curriculum Guidance for the Foundation Stage.* London: Qualifications and Curriculum Authority.

Ranzoni, P. (1973) *Considerations in Developing an Outside Area for Schools/Centers for Young Children.* Orano: University of Maine.

Richards, R. (1983) 'Learning through science', in Blenkin, G. M. and Kelly, A. V. (eds) *The Primary Curriculum in Action.* London: Harper and Row.

Robson, M. and Hunt, K. (1999) 'An innovative approach to involving parents in the education of their early years children', *International Journal of Early Years Education* **7**(2), 185–93.

Robson, S. (1996) 'The physical environment', in Robson, S. and Smedley, S. (eds) *Education in Early Childhood*, 153–71. London: David Fulton Publishers.

Singer, D. and Singer, J. (1990) *The House of Make-Believe: Play and the Developing Imagination.* Cambridge, MA: Harvard University Press.

Smilansky, S. and Shefatya, L. (1990) *Facilitating Play: A Medium for Promoting Cognitive, Socio-Emotional and Academic Development in Young Children.* Gaithersburg, MD: Psychosocial and Educational Publications.

Smith, P. K. and Connelly, K. J. (1981) *The Ecology of Pre-School Behaviour.* Cambridge: Cambridge University Press.

Sports Council (1992) *Allied Dunbar National Fitness Survey. A Summary.* London: The Sports Council and the Health Education Authority.

Steedman, C. (1990) *Childhood, Culture and Class in Britain: Margaret McMillan, 1860–1931.* London: Virago.

Stevenson, C. (1987) 'The young four year old in nursery and infant classes: challenges and constraints', in *Four Year Olds in School. Policy and Practice*, 34–43. Slough: NFER/SCDC.

Stewart, D. (1989) 'Forward role', *The Times Educational Supplement*, 21 April, B2.

Sugden, D. and Wright, H. (1996) 'Curricular entitlement and implementation for all children', in Armstrong, N. (ed.) *New Directions in Physical Education. Change and Innovation*, 110–30. London: Cassell.

Sylva, K., Roy, C., Painter, M. (1980) *Child Watching at Playgroup and Nursery School.* London: Grant McIntyre.

Szreter, R. (1964) 'The origins of full-time compulsory schooling at five', *British Journal of Educational Studies* **XIII**, 1.

Taylor, B. J. (1980) 'Pathways to a healthy self-concept', in Yaroke, T. D. (ed.) *The Self Concept of the Young Child.* Salt Lake City: Brigham Young Press.

Taylor, P. H., Exon, G., Holley, B. (1972) *A Study of Nursery Education.* London: Evans/Methuen Educational.

Teets, S. T. (1985) 'Modification of play behaviors of preschool children through manipulation of environmental variables', in Frost, J. L. and Sunderlin, S. (eds) *When Children Play. Proceedings of the International Conference on Play and Play Environments*, 265–71. Wheaton, MD: Association for Childhood Education International.

Tizard, B., Philps, J., Plewis, I. (1976a) 'Play in pre-school centres – I. Play measures and their relation to age, sex and IQ', *Journal of Child Psychology and Psychiatry* **17**, 251–64.

Tizard, B., Philps, J., Plewis, I. (1976b) 'Play in pre-school centres – II. Effects on play of the child's social class and of the educational orientation of the centre', *Journal of Child Psychology and Psychiatry* **17**, 265–74.

Tizard, B., Philps, J., Plewis, I. (1977) 'Staff behaviour in pre-school centres', *Journal of Child Psychology and Psychiatry* **18,** 21–33.

Trevarthen, C. (1994) *How Children Learn Before School*. Lecture Text. London: British Association for Early Childhood Education, 2 November.

Vygotsky, L. (1978) *Mind in Society*. Cambridge, MA: Harvard University Press.

Walkerdine, V. (1996) 'Girls and boys in the classroom', in Pollard, A. (ed.) *Readings for Reflective Teaching in the Primary School*, 298–300. London: Cassell.

Walsh, P. (1993) 'Fixed equipment – a time for change', *Australian Journal of Early Childhood* **18**(2), 23–9.

Webb, L. (1974) *Purpose and Practice in Nursery Education*. Oxford: Blackwell.

Wells, G. (1987) *The Meaning Makers. Children Learning Language and Using Language to Learn*. London: Hodder & Stoughton.

Wetton, P. (1983) 'Some observations of interest in locomotor and gross motor activity in nursery schools', *PE Review* **6**(2), 124–9.

Wetton, P. (1988) *Physical Education in the Nursery and Infant School*. London: Routledge.

Wetton, P. (1998) 'Physical development in the early years', in Siraj-Blatchford, I. (ed.) *A Curriculum Development Handbook for Early Childhood Educators*. Stoke on Trent: Trentham Books Limited.

Whalley, M. (1996) 'Working as a team', in Pugh, G. (ed.) *Contemporary Issues in the Early Years*, 2nd edn. London: Paul Chapman Publishing.

Wheeler, O. and Earl, I. (1939) *Nursery School Education and the Re-organization of the Infant School*. London: University of London Press.

Whitbread, N. (1972) *The Evolution of the Nursery-Infant School*. London: Routledge and Kegan Paul.

Whitehurst, J. (2001) 'How the development of high quality outside areas for reception children can promote play and personal, social and emotional learning'.Unpublished MA dissertation, University of Hertfordshire.

Whyte, J. (1983) *Beyond the Wendy House: Sex Role Stereotyping in Primary Schools*. York: Longmans for Schools Council.

Wood, D. (1988) *How Children Think and Learn*. Oxford: Blackwell.

Wood, E. and Attfield, J. (1996) *Play, Learning and the Early Childhood Curriculum*. London: Paul Chapman Publishing.

Wood, L. and Bennett, N. (1997) 'The rhetoric and reality of play: teachers' thinking and classroom practice', *Early Years* **17**(2), 22–7.

Wragg, E. C. (1993) *Class Management*. London: Routledge.

Wragg, T. (1997) 'Oh Boy!', *The Times Educational Supplement* **2**, 16 May, 4–5.

Yerkes, R. (1982) A playground that extends the classroom.

Zaichkowsky, L. D., Zaichkowsky, L. B., Martinek, T. J. (1980) *Growth and Development: The Child and Physical Activity*. London: C V Mosby.

Index

Printed in the United Kingdom
by Lightning Source UK Ltd.
110478UKS00001B/389-452